T0209712

TIME TO AWAKEN AND HEAL

THE AWAKENING JOURNEY TO WHO YOU ARE

Lois Cunningham

BALBOA.
PRESS
A DIVISION OF HAY HOUSE

Balboa Press books may be ordered through booksellers or by contacting:

Balboa Press
A Division of Hay House
1663 Liberty Drive
Bloomington, IN 47403
www.balboapress.com
1 (877) 407-4847

Print information available on the last page.

ISBN: 978-1-9822-3183-5 (sc)
ISBN: 978-1-9822-3197-2 (e)

Balboa Press rev. date: 07/22/2019

CONTENTS

This book is my journey and my understanding of experiences I have had. This is my Disclaimer. I suggest everyone do their own research on information I share. Take on board what resonates with you and please feel free to discard the rest. You are not alone, there are millions of us Starseeds incarnated on Mother Earth at this time in history. Many of us volunteered to be here at this time but only few of us were chosen! We are the chosen ones!

I am on FB and am finding that I am connecting with many other Starseeds and Soul Family, this gives me so much joy as we were scattered all over Mother Earth so we could be safe. It has been a very lonely existence feeling that we didn't fit in, many of us are the "Black Sheep" of the family, feeling like square pegs in round holes. Now is the time to remember who we are and why we have come here and what our mission / purpose here is.

RESOURCES I HAVE FOUND USEFUL IN MY RECOVERY ARE

Doing your Inner Child Work with a person who specialises in this area! I wish I could tell you this healing is something you could do in a weekend but that would be an outright lie!

For many of you it has taken you decades to get to this place of "Crash and Burn" so you are now ready to do your Healing Process. Release ALL JUDGEMENTS you have of yourself and others!

There is a saying that says," Nothing happens until the time is right"!

We need to take baby steps, sometimes three steps forward and two steps backwards! All this Emotional damage is like an onion with many layers beginning in our childhood. Of course, when we begin our Healing journey we need to start on the outside layers of that onion, whatever is currently happening in your life and work our way back to the beliefs we took on board as a child which have manifested throughout our lives. Most importantly, please, be gentle with yourselves! Remember, you were just doing the best you could with the tools you had at the time. The same goes for our parents who raised us the best way they could with the tools and understanding they had!

During my journey I came across an amazing lady by the name of Melanie Tonia Evans who suffered severely from Narcissistic Abuse herself, nearly dying from it!

Melanie has created many different resources which have been acknowledged as very effective by Professionals in the field of recovery from Emotional and Physical abuse. Melanie has done many You Tube videos which are extremely informative. For Empaths at the beginning of their recovery she has put together a free starter package for your Healing Journey:

https://www.melanietoniaevans.com/freestarterpackage.htm.
Please feel free to check this out!

She has written a book called, You can thrive after Narcissistic Abuse.

Melanie also has a FB Page, where she shares about her Narcissistic Abuse Recovery Program which has been said to be the number one system for recovering from toxic relationships.

She mentions that the Thriver accepts that their previous trauma exposed what was as yet not whole within.

Melanie holds Webinars and is the Founder of Quanta Freedom Healing and the Narcissistic Abuse.

Here are two other resources to connect with Melanie:
www.melanietoniaevans.com and support@melanietoniaevans.com

Melanie offers a free 16 day Recovery Course as well.

Melanie also has a Blog which is: BLOG.MELANIETONIA EVANS.COM

Melanie also creates Thriver TV Episodes.

INTRODUCTION

Thou shall awaken to who thou art for it is only in the awareness will you realise your worth as many volunteered but few were chosen.

We are the ones who were the chosen to do this sacred task. We have taken this on as we have done many lifetimes before. We were scattered far and wide, and feel so alone, but thanks to the internet we are now reconnecting with other members of our Soul Family.

I believe the best way to help the Planet is by working on ourselves! That way we can be the living example for others. This is what I hope to achieve by sharing my story with you!

I would like to share my background with you so you can understand the story of my life with a clearer understanding of where my beliefs have originated from.

I am a Starseed, Lightworker, Psychic, Empath, Counsellor, Healing channel (Hollow Bone, as the Healing Energy comes through, us not from us), and a Spiritualist so what I share with you comes from all these aspects of me. I need to explain this so you can understand my belief systems and make it easier for you to follow what I am saying.

My job is to be a LIVING EXAMPLE for those who don't know how to.

This book is my contribution to other STARSEEDS that will recognise my journey and know it is the same for them! We have incarnated here for many lifetimes except for the Walk Ins and those for whom this is their first lifetime. Believe it or not, we

VOLUNTEERED to be here to assist Humanity and Mother Earth to ascend into the 5th dimension experience. It is my belief that many of us have assisted other planets to ascend, Mother Earth is the last one to go through this process in this sector so there is great interest with other races who are now surrounding and observing us. It is my understanding that the Pleiadians were given permission on the 17th November 2017 to step in and assist humanity with this process as there are many service to self entities (negative) who are trying their hardest to stop Ascention occurring, they have been successful in the past but not this time! This is my understanding!

For those of you who are unfamiliar with what a Starseed is I will share some references for you to explore.

You Tube has some excellent videos, some examples of these are:

Which Alien Starseed are you? (Pleiadian, Sirian, etc.) This video is created by Stargirl, the practical witch.

What is your Galactic Origin is a video from the book, Where are you really from? By Jo Amidon

Another video is 20 signs you are a Starseed.

This is just a jumping off platform for you to explore further.

CHAPTER ONE

Background Information

Personally I was very reluctant to come this time around. I had a very interesting experience with one person I was working with energetically in a training course, we were told to tune into major traumas with each other and he picked up a dark entity waiting for me to be born!

My mother was in labour for 36 hours. After giving birth to two children myself, I developed a deep compassion for what my mother had experienced. I tried to exit stage left, in other words I was dying, but got sent back down here. I tried to change my mind but was unsuccessful. I was reminded I had a contract to fulfil.

My father who is Catholic, had a Mass said for me, apparently I began to get stronger and healthier after the Mass was said. As an incarnating Soul, I thought I had placed too much on my plate. My Guides needed to remind me that I chose to do this, as we all choose to come here. In my understanding, this is a School of Life where we come to learn lessons such as Patience, Trust, Surrender, etc., and learn how to listen to our intuition, (which is how our Angels / Guides, communicate with us). I needed to step out of Victim mode.

I have reincarnated many times and I am aware we only grow through the pain of lessons that we set up for ourselves, on a Soul level, for our own Personal Growth! It would be nice if we could grow Spiritually through Peace and Harmony but sadly that is not the case.

We need to crash and burn before the pain gives us the strength to change what we are experiencing.

A gentle reminder was given to me recently to enjoy my Humanness, very appropriate as I focus a lot of my attention on my Sky Family. They help and support me every day, in many ways, and I am extremely grateful to them. I literally put my life in their hands, as I totally believe they will make sure I complete the mission I came here to fulfil.

I was born in Geelong, Victoria, Australia. My father was a farm hand so for the first three years of my life we moved from farm to farm. My mother would dress us in red tracksuits, it was many decades before I could wear red again. Fussy lady just wanted to be able to see us out on the land bless her. I had no idea why I had such a dislike for it until Mum explained to me decades later.

My mother was the first female bio-chemist at Griffiths Sweets, quite an achievement indeed for that period of time! I am so proud of her!

The first place I remember living was Skipton. I tried to teach a chicken to swim in a 44 gallon drum and was very disappointed when it couldn't. I was three years old. I thought the chickens were ducklings and could not understand why it didn't swim, poor wee chicken. My father stepped on one and my sister who was only two years old, hugged one very tightly. Those poor chicks had very short lives.

There was a young girl who lived down the road who had this amazing doll house. To us, that doll house was extremely impressive, we had never seen anything so fancy. Obviously it left a massive impression on my mind because sixty years later, I still remember being so amazed by it. My current self has come to the conclusion she must have been the farmer's daughter.

My sister's cot and mine were put together. She would climb into my cot so easily but I had to struggle very hard to climb into hers! It is such a vivid memory like it was just yesterday. I must admit, I was so perplexed why I was having such difficulty! There was a very good reason for that as I was born with Talipes; my feet were twisted inwards and there were many trips to the Royal Children hospital in Tramville. I remember those long corridors with the seats against the walls.

I would always, so it seemed, get car sick as we were leaving Swantown, Woodman's Hill seemed to be my favourite place to vomit, must have been nerves as I knew where I was going and there would be pain. Never been good at pain, a very low pain threshold, unlike other members of my family. Mum suffered severe migraines unfortunately, I couldn't even handle a headache. Interestingly I never got car sick when we were going to see family in Geelong, only when I was going to the Children's Hospital in Tramville.

I was three years old when we left Skipton to live in Swantown where my parents would buy the home. As they had grown up during the Depression, they had experienced much lack and struggle in their lives so it was an important dream of theirs to own their own home. Somewhere I still have the book they noted the payments they made on the house. Of course, back then it was in Pounds, Shillings and Pence. My mother had a purse of her mother's which actually contained half penny's and farthings.

I remember going to the Milk Bar when I was at Primary school and being able to buy four lollies for a penny, I think they may have been freckles. Cobblers and spearmint leaves were also common. I loved Musk sticks, white knights and Chew chew bars, they were rather more expensive. Mint patties were also one of my favourites. In later years when Wagon Wheels came in they were huge, nothing like present day, I quite fancied them as well but I am digressing. How many of you took a trip down lolly memory lane with me then?

I grew up in a poor area of Swantown, Wendouree West, it is a Ministry of Housing area where most people rented their homes, like now. Our street, Banksia Road was for people buying their own homes so I found out decades later.

My parents both worked very hard. They both grew up during the Depression and so to own their own home was very important to them. As a result, we were minded by other people until our parents picked us up after work, there were no creches or Family Day Care facilities way back then. As we got older we became "Latch key kids", home alone doing chores such as cooking dinner for our parents so it would be ready when they got home.

We had a black and white cat, he loved sitting on the wood pile around our garage, his name was Woody! I wonder where he got that name from, I say this with a massive smile on my face because I can still see him in my mind, sunning himself on the massive wood pile we had. We had a combustion stove and Dad would make a "stoke" of the wood in the stove. If it happened to go out we would have to go next door and get Nanny Egelton to light the fire for us, she was a beautiful sweet and kind, lady. Woody liked sleeping in the vegetable garden also, Mum and Dad weren't too thrilled when he would go in there. Hey cats love digging holes, it comes naturally to them!

Our other next door neighbour had an German Shepard dog called Penny. To us she was so big we were terrified of her. Mum and Dad decided to buy a Welsh Corgi so we could become comfortable around dogs. Another reason for getting a Welsh Corgi, was to assist in bringing the cows up to the shed to have their hay, while we were milking them. Later on dad bought a Queensland blue Heeler, her name was Lady, mum didn't seem to like her because when we went on a camping trip to Tasmania she gave her away to be used for chemical testing, dad was not happy about that! Dad sold our cows shortly afterwards. Madge was a beautiful gentle Jersey, Beauty was a very nervous Ayrshire. Beauty's horns were so big she picked me up and carried me for some distance once. She didn't hurt me however. I was trying to bring her up for milking and she wanted to play with the bull. I was terrified of the bull, he was normally in the next paddock. Even after all this time I could still milk a cow by hand, oh boy, my hands would cramp at time but the udder would be lovely and warm during the cold months. Bringing the cows up to the shed for milking was not always an easy task, finding them on such a massive Common with so many trees to hide under. Madge was pretty easy to bring up but Beauty kept trying to turn around and go back up the common so we would have to chase her. We were only in Primary school at the time and cows can run fast which is where Candy came in useful.

Our first Welsh Corgi we named Goldie, due to the colour of her coat of course. We had an outside toilet at that time, and a potty under our beds for night time. We were only young and going outside in the dark and with the cold and wet Swantown weather just was not going to happen. The potties were a pale green and round on the sides with a lip around the edge and a handle.

Anyway rats and mice were an issue, so Dad put down some poison for them. Sadly Goldie must have eaten one, the poison killed her. I clearly remember her pleading eyes asking me to help her so I told Dad she was sick. Dad told me she would be fine, in the morning she was dead and buried up on the Common. I was mad at dad for lying to me and grieved deeply for Goldie, blaming myself for not being able to save her. I was in the lower Primary school grades at the time. I searched the common to find her grave, I found her on the banks of the creek, near the Pine trees she loved playing under. Her grave looked so small but the rectangular shape gave it away. I can still see it in my mind. Even sixty years later I still weep when I speak of her loss, my Inner Child seems to sneak to the surface.

Several months later Mum and Dad got another Welsh Corgi, I wanted to call her Goldie as well but my parents insisted she had another name so we settled on Candy. I formed a very strong bond with Candy believing Goldie had come back to be with me. I would take Candy out for regular walks. I would talk to Candy like she was human, she was very intelligent, she understood me well. How many of you do this with your fur babies? When I was sad she would comfort me. Our fur babies never judge or criticise us, they just give us unconditional love and are extremely faithful to us unlike a lot of humans.

When I went into the Nurses Home to begin my Nursing Career, Candy took herself off for a walk and got hit by a car and was killed. Once again I was filled with grief for her. I had abandoned her, nobody else seemed to take her for walks, that had been my job! When I was learning to drive I remember dad saying to me, if there is an animal on the road it is better to hit the animal than possibly cause the death or injury of a human because you swerved onto the other side of the road. Personally I would rather toot the horn and hit the brakes. I could never hit an animal if I could manage to avoid it.

Due to my father's past, we grew a vegetable garden with a wide variety such as corn, beans, peas, carrots, beetroot, cabbage (chasing those cabbage moths was a frequent exercise we did as we didn't want them eating our cabbages!) Dad would plant several rows of each vegetable and change them each season. One of our chores was weeding the garden, I still remember feeling so dizzy bending over for so long. I found out later I had a low blood pressure like my father. A special treat for the cows was the corn stems. We had had chickens in cages so we could keep track of who was laying, only one chook per cage of course. There was a book with each number of the cages, we had to put a stroke next to each cage number that had laid an egg, the fifth stroke of course, went across the other four just to make counting easier. Whoever stopped laying became roast chicken for dinner. We had a hay shed, climbing those square bales of hay was a scratchy experience.

We would go out to collect the wood for our combustion stove. I remember well those trips to the bush for firewood where our 1952 Vanguard would pull a trailer with very high sides on it that we would climb up on. I remember my sister and I following a track, it faded out and then we realised we were lost so we just listened for the sound of the axe and followed it back to our parents.

My mother loved lists and as we grew up we were given chores to do from the time we woke up to the time we went to bed, seven days a week. We were given pocket money as long as we balanced our book correctly. Occasionally the stoke on the combustion stove would go out so we would have to go next door to Nanny Eggelton and get her to come and assist us to get it going again. It was our job to have the dinner cooked by the time our parents came home from work. And yes, we prepared the vegetables from the garden before we went to school.

My sister always washed the dishes, it was my job to dry them and put them away! Interesting how that affected me as an adult! Dishes would pile up in the sink because my sister wasn't there to wash them, it was bizarre. When Mum and Dad came to visit Mum would often wash my dishes. In my defence I was absolutely exhausted getting up six, even seven times a night to feed or change babies. I really don't perform very well when I haven't had enough sleep. I am not one of those people who survive fine on 5 hours sleep, I need a minimum of 8 hours to function properly. I am sure I am not the only one with this issue.

I have been a "Loner" for many years. I was born with Talipes, my feet were twisted inward, as a result I wore Calipers up until I began school. I was still wearing them when I went to Kindergarten. I remember so clearly nobody wanted to play with me. When I was an adult I asked Mum why I had no playmates when I was there. Mum explained to me I had begun Kindergarten in the third term so everyone had already formed their friendships and that I looked weird to the other kids due to wearing the Calipers.

My father is a catholic, my mother belonged to the Church of Christ. I was the result of a one night stand, dad was engaged to another lady but my parents met at Square dancing. I am so proud of my mother, she refused to become a catholic even though dad's parents put a lot of pressure on her. Mum told Dad she would leave if we went to catholic school so we went to State School. During Religious Education we had to leave the room. Dad did not want us to get ant Protestant religious education. This of course made us stand out from the rest of the children. I remember helping my sister learn how to read during this period where we were sent to the Office. The grade two teacher was the headmistress and also a catholic. Her and her sister became our sponsors for confirmation. Dad would take us to Mass every Sunday, in those days we had to wear head coverings, mantilas or hats. We were dressed in our Sunday best. The mass was said in Latin, I knew all the responses! I had absolutely no idea what the English translation was however. Just a side note here, recently there was a video on You Tube of a mass being said in Latin and they were worshipping Lucifer! Of course the congregation had absolutely no idea that was what they were doing. For twenty five years David Icke has been exposing the Luciferian presence in the upper ranks of the Secret Societies, Freemasons and the Catholic religion. Don't take my word for it, DO YOUR OWN RESEARCH!

.I did have one friend in Primary school who also had long hair and plaits. I met up with her and her husband at Gympie when they were towing their caravans from Swantown, with their neighbours. She has lived in Swantown all her life.

Something else really major was going on during this time, the thirty year war in Ireland between the Catholics and Protestants. The catholic kids would throw stones at us, the war came all the way over to Australia. Of course stones would be thrown back and kids got hurt, it was sad to see and terrifying to be caught in the middle of. The only thing that united the Irish was their hate of the English soldiers on their roofs who were playing "Peace keepers".

As I got older I really questioned the division within Christianity, they all seemed to have their own version of the bible, it just didn't make any sense to me! As I got older I became aware of the existence of other religions and I began to question what could possibly be a common denominator between ALL religions and Atheists as well. My conclusion was that no matter what your Belief, Race, Colour, Nationality or shoe size, we are ALL children of God! Now I do not believe God is a Human Being or an Extra Terrestrial for that matter, I believe God is Spirit. Now this belief was cemented within my mind when I heard of the experiments Elizabeth Kubler Ross was doing with people who were dying. She had them on scales and noted a difference in their weight after they died, they were lighter and her conclusion was this was due to the Soul leaving the body.

I am a Spiritualist, I believe we are all Spirit having a Human experience in this School of Duality, learning lessons, rather than a human with a Soul. We were Spirit before we incarnated and became human, taking on this flesh overcoat, when we take off this flesh overcoat, we are still Spirit! I totally agree with the Lakota Sioux Native Americans, they use a saying Mitakuye Oyasin, WE ARE ONE! I am so over all the false divisions that have been created in the world today so the Illuminati can spin us a story and get us to hate each other or be so Patriotic that we are willing to go to war to kill each other while the Reserve Bank get rich through backing BOTH SIDES of EVERY WAR! :(David Icke has been telling us this for 25 years!

However I have digressed just a tad, back to my childhood.

Discipline was extremely strict, we got the strap and electric cord which was very harsh but my father was belted with the horse whip. I vowed I would never hit my children with any object so they got my hand on their bottoms which hurt me as well as them. How things have changed! I feared my father as he was the disciplinarian. So many kids now a days don't seem to have any respect what so ever for their parents. Giving them time out or sending them to their rooms, does it really work? With what I have seen with my Grandchildren verbal abuse seems to have replaced physical abuse and that is way more damaging as the subconscious mind fails to differentiate between Truth and a Lie. Whatever is constantly said to a child becomes their inner voice and their reality. As a result there are many verbally abused children with very low self-esteem who keep repeating patterns of "I don't deserve", for example, right through their adult lives. It is very important for these children to do their Inner Child work and Emotionally heal.

My understanding of why we are here

I believe that on a Soul level we choose our parents before we incarnate. Often times we Reincarnate with the same family playing different roles. Those of us who are psychic had to spend a lot of time withdrawn into ourselves because that is where it was safe, so we maintained our connection to Spirit. When there is no chaos or abuse in your life you have no reason to go within so often the connection with Spirit is lost.

We also need to remember that on a physical, 3rd dimensional reality, our parents raise us to the best of their ability. Sadly

Generational patterns are often just reproduced because Society says our parents "Love" us. Sadly this "Love "is often, chaos, abuse, abandonment and neglect. Happily sometimes children do get tender loving care and support as "Love". This is the love of Romance Novels that we all crave. What we need to understand is that the first 7 years of our life is where our "Love Equation" is formed. It is very important to understand our parents probably followed the parenting pattern of their own parents. We can hold anger at our parents for decades for how we were treated, we can find it extremely hard to Forgive them for what they did or failed to do. Remember, they did the best they knew how to do! And yes, we did choose, on a Soul level to have them as our parents!

When we don't Forgive, remember it has absolutely no effect on the person we are not forgiving, but it destroys OUR MENTAL, EMOTIONAL and even PHYSICAL health so the reasons we Forgive has NOTHING to do with them, it has EVERYTHING to do with us and OUR HEALTH! What I have found very useful when dealing with Forgiveness is to work with one person at a time, maybe the easiest one first, then gradually working up to the most challenging. I suggest to my clients to safely burn a candle, like in the middle of a table, making sure there is NOTHING FLAMMABLE around it! Hand write a letter to whoever it is you need to forgive! Write your anger out, the same sentence over and over, cry, yell scream, get that pain out!!What I need you to understand is that these people are purely ACTORS, playing a part that on a Soul level, you asked them to play so you could learn the lesson!

Now lessons can be difficult to discover / understand. It may be Patience, Trust, Surrender, Listening to Spirit for example.

A tool I found very useful when you are working through Anger is just to keep writing! It doesn't need to make sense! It can be the one sentence over and over again, a thousand times if necessary! Just keep going until you are feeling calmer within yourself! Some people, and children, would find it easier to draw a picture of what is making them angry and upset! Yes, you can just scribble all over the page also, a brilliant release! I have found that burning a candle while you are doing this very good for cleansing the atmosphere! Just keep it very far away from anything flammable because that candle will shoot up very high!

Look at using crystals and incense and essential oils to keep you calm as well. The Narcissist loves upsetting you, your misery is their joy!

I recommend after you have released all your anger, take one page at a time and burn it over the toilet bowl, after lifting the plastic seat preferably! We don't need to damage that! This creates a safe environment to burn the letter. Make sure you have some bleach to clean the toilet bowl afterwards! Make sure you have plenty of tissues to wipe your tears and blow your noses. Screaming into a pillow or winding the windows up in the car and scream but ONLY while the car is parked!

CHAPTER TWO

Flying the Coop

The year after I matriculated I began my Nursing Career. In those days we went into the Nurses Quarters and lived in small rooms but at least it was handy to work! I am pleased I had that experience. It was in the hospital grounds so it took like 10 minutes to get to work, depending on where the Ward was and how long you had to wait for the lift. I wore a hat, a button up dress that had removable buttons and a purple cape to keep me warm. We wore stockings also, no socks. They would starch our uniforms, they could stand up on their own sometimes. I still remember how the peg of the buttons would scratch you and often put holes on your stockings, really not a very comfortable uniform. Swantown was so cold on many occasions and those capes, even though they looked very bright, didn't really keep the cold out very well, especially on those frosty Winter mornings. We were given a new Ward every 8 weeks and worked three late shifts then seven early shifts. Those "suicide" shifts I would call them really exhausted me and that was on the first of the seven morning shifts, I was so exhausted come the last one.

The first Ward I worked on was the Children's Ward. Just between you, me and the yonder gate post, I was terrified of telling people what to do. I was so relieved to be dealing with children on my first Ward. I did sixteen weeks in Women's Medical; Sister Brown was very strict and scary. My mother kept coming up to the Ward because I would head down to Bridge Street as soon as I got off work so she could never catch up with me. I was free at last and was making the most of my freedom!

I did eight weeks in Women's Surgical. That was the Ward I was doing the drips, Reports, Hand Overs, injections. I must admit I felt a tad overwhelmed, it was a lot of responsibility for a Year One nurse. Mind you, they were afternoon shifts.

I got to remove sutures when I was working in Emergency which was the last place I worked at that hospital. I quite enjoyed Emergency, there was such a variety. That was the last Ward I did before I left Swantown Base Hospital. For my first lot of holidays, my girlfriend and I did a first class tour for our holidays. We were so clueless that First Class meant retired grey brigade. We were so shocked when we realised we were the only young ones on the tour. We were so relieved when we arrived at Eden and that lovely Ambulance driver joined us. That really made a massive difference to our holiday. Made a lot of interesting memories.

The next year my sister and I moved to Tramville as my sister had been accepted into Monash University and my parents would not let her go on her own. Our parents bought her a little yellow Mini Minor which she drove it with bare feet. I could not believe how tiny those pedals were! I was convinced there was no way someone with shoes on could drive it. It was a manual. The sole of a shoe would cover all three pedals! I have great admiration for anyone who drove those cars!

My parents brought Sandy, the nurse I did the holiday with, to Tramville for my 21st birthday, that was an amazing celebration. Sandy was on night shift so she slept in the car on the way to Tramville. My mother's sister in law was extremely creative and made me an amazing 21st Birthday cake, I still have photos of that cake and all that came to celebrate with me. I was in a relationship with Rudy at that time. I had a very memorable 21st and was so deeply grateful to my parents, Auntie and Uncle for all the effort they went to for it. Rudy is Dutch, my mother wore a navy blue Kaftan with tulips all over it, we even had a pot of tulips on the kitchen table.

I continued training and became a Nurse Aide working mainly in Geriatric hospitals for many years. I even got to nurse in New Zealand at Rawhiti Private Trust Hospital in Mount Eden in Auckland. I could see the tree on One tree Hill from my room window. Starting work at 6 a.m. took a bit of getting used to, I must admit! My fiancé had to go back to work in Australia. I went back to Australia three times before I finally went home for good.

My massive overseas journey in 1976

I ended up going overseas to England, Scandinavia, Russia, Europe, Portugal, Spain and Morocco. I went with Atrek Tours who were based in Clapham South. It was a big house we all stayed in before our tours left and between tours. I went on the London buses and the underground! Oh man, the different colours helped but all the levels were so confusing. I did check it out very well while I was there. Of course I had to go up to the top of a double decker bus! The underground didn't give you much of a view of the suburbs, funny about that. I went over during their Summer, from memory I think it was one of the hottest they had ever had which suited me well, I don't do cold very well even though I grew up with frost and sleet.

My first trip was a 44 day Scandinavia / Russia Tour, I then did a 42 day tour of North Africa including Spain and Portugal. Good thing I saved my travel brochure and wrote a diary so I can share some of my highlights with you, after all, that was 43 years ago, lol.

I hired a bike in Amsterdam, those cobblestone roads took a toll on me for several days afterwards, it was painful sitting but I am so pleased I had the experience. Having to think in reverse turning corners was rather exciting, I am glad I wasn't trying to drive a car. Finding our way to the Heiniken Brewery was quite the adventure. I was pleased there were several of us on the bikes.

Visiting Anne Frank's House was incredible! You needed a chain saw to cut through the atmosphere all those years later! Gee those staircases are so small I could only place the ball of my foot on it, a bit scary climbing them as I am used to being able to place my whole foot on the step. Seeing the bookcase was so emotional knowing that was the only thing keeping Anne Frank, her family and the others safe from the Germans. I didn't understand why I was so sensitive to the energy. At that stage I didn't understand I was an Empath; I knew nothing about Psychic abilities.

I was surprised to see they had trams in Amsterdam like they do in Tramville. Of course I had to get a photo of myself in National Costume in Volendam. Yes, I even bought a pair of wooden clogs which I kept for decades, only released them when I could no longer fit my feet into them. Another memory was seeing a chimp dressed in shorts and a shirt climbing in through the window of a Combi Van, there were heaps of those we saw on our travels.

Berlin was a very interesting place energetically, once again the atmosphere was so thick. We visited the Escape Museum then went through Check Point Charlie into East Berlin. It was so heartbreaking, families were separated by that wall and many died trying to escape. I was so overjoyed years later when the wall came down! Going through Check Point Charlie was so tense, extremely strict, never forget that feeling!

I was so thrilled to get letters from my mother and sister when I arrived in Denmark, it meant so much to me. I have kept those aerogram letters also. I couldn't believe how small the Little Mermaid was expected her to be much larger. Saw and experienced snow for the first time in Norway, one of the guys decided to put snow down my back, so thoughtful of him, A highlight of Norway was going out on a fishing boat and getting to catch our own lunch, I contributed a large fish and was the first one of the girls to catch a fish. They cooked them on board the boat for us. In Sweden we visited the Wasa Museum, an old Swedish Warship that had sunk. There were American Tourists asking how could they afford to sell the, made in Taiwan, replicas of things that were found on board. It did not seem to occur to them that hello, they only looked like the original.

I quickly learned to let people know I was not American as they charge the American Tourists double of what we were charged. I mean it really made me wonder, all they had to do was turn the article over and see the made in Taiwan sticker on the bottom of it. It had been raised again in 1961.

Another thing in Scandinavia that really was quite challenging is that there are no private cubicles in the shower, quite confronting. How to lose your hangups in one easy lesson. Interesting how that loss of inhibition stayed with me for a long time. Helsinki was very beautiful with lots of parks. I got another two letters from my Mum and another one from my sister, it feels really good having news from home.

The camp site in Finland was amongst a whole heap of trees. The idea of experiencing 24 hours of daylight was mind blowing so I stayed up a most of the night to immerse myself thoroughly into that experience! A once in a lifetime experience being able to walk around at night like it was just dusk and being able to see all the tree roots so you didn't trip over them! I stayed up till 4am, woke at 6am and slept into Russia. It was a very lengthy experience getting through the Russian Border, keeping in mind, the Black Market was very active selling jeans and the KGB was constantly watching everyone, especially the tourists and their Guides.

We went into Palace Square. They have trolley buses as well as trams there. Seeing old women dressed in black with straw brooms sweeping the street was such a haunting memory. The energy of Russia for me was grey. They do mass weddings in Russia, a hundred people or so all getting married at the same time, it seems to be compulsory for them all to go to a War Memorial or Tanks of some sort after the wedding, they connect it with Russian strength and pride in their country. Moscow (Mockba) has the best vanilla ice-cream in the world I believe! They sell it as a cream between two wafers, it was truly divine, very memorable. I certainly did not expect that from a Communist Country which I saw as backwards at that time. Everywhere there were lines of people waiting at shops with no advertising on the windows, you had no idea, as a Westerner, what was being sold in there, no advertising whatsoever!

We spend one and three quarter hours waiting in line to go

through Lenin's Tomb, another interesting energy! It is compulsory for everyone to visit his tomb on a regular basis, from memory I think it was every three months but it was a long time ago and I may be wrong. One vision that sums up Russia is the queues, little plain buildings, butchers, backers, there was absolutely no sign on the shop to tell you what it was! Red Square was very impressive with the variety of architecture of the surrounding buildings. Equality of sexes seems to be normal here in Russia, women as well as men work on the road crews. Children are raised by the Communist State while their parents work.

We spent three hours going through Russian Customs into Romania where we had to spend a compulsory amount of money, minimum, per day. I noted these people seemed much happier and much more colourful than the Russians. There are no fences so the children mind the cattle. We crossed the Danube into Bulgaria and drove down Elton John's "Yellow Brick Road", literally, it was made of yellow bricks, yeah, I was surprised also! It is in Sofia. Lots of donkeys here.

We crossed into Turkey. Crazy drivers here, always blowing their horns. Horses and carts combine with the cars. We went to a huge bazar and tried our hand at bargaining. It covered 114 acres and contained 5,000 shops, immense to say the least, very easy to get lost in! I bought a leather coat there and went out with the guy I bought the coat from, arriving back at camp just half an hour before the bus left, that was a close shave! He wanted me to stay! Was awarded the "Booby prize" for staying out the night before. This was awarded to the person who did the silliest thing each day, I deserved it. Was so thankful I got back in time. The easiest way for Turkish men to come to Australia is to marry an Australian woman so of course he asked me to marry him. He wanted to come to Tramville and set up a business with the leather there.

So good to receive 3 more letters from home. We experienced a Turkish bath but somehow missed out on the massage. Visiting the graves at Gallipoli was a real eye opener as most of the dead were in their late teens, early 20s. I did find a grave of a 16 year old. The boys were putting their ages up so they could fight for their country, so sad to see all those young lives lost so the Reserve Bank could make some more money, so tragic! They back both sides of EVERY WAR by the way!

We passed into Greece, they have Travellers boxes here that contain food and water. I found that quite fascinating! Saw part of the original Roman road, more cobbled roads here. Saw where the Olympic flame originated. I just love the Greek tradition of having a siesta during the day, much like the Mexicans. Visiting Pompei was pretty mind blowing, feeling the fear and seeing ashen covered bodies so well preserved. I noticed a lot of Bambina cars here, they also like using their horns but not as much as in Turkey. Visited Mount Vesuvious, talk about the smell of sulphur!

September 9th is Rudy's birthday and also the day my parents moved from my childhood home. The reason I did the trip was to run away from the memory of Rudy and the abortion he made me have. He promised me he would stay with me if I "Got rid of the kid", his words. I was so jealous and possessive of him, I did what he wanted. The things you do when you are young, we were engaged and getting married was extremely important to me! I suffered severe depression after the abortion and tried to commit suicide, Rudy left me at the hospital. Hormone imbalance really mess with your head severely.

When I was younger, in Primary school, we use to get sent away or Mum would go away for a break. She was very highly strung. One of the places we use to be sent was down to Geelong to a beautiful old lady who had a big car, we called her Gran Mac Cleese. Being the eldest child it felt like I was always being blamed for everything that went wrong. As a Counsellor I would refer to this as playing the role of "Blame Post". We all play roles to get attention and this is the role I seemed to have taken on. As a result of this self-imposed role, which I wasn't consciously aware of, I understand now I suffered from severe Depression. On a Soul level I chose to do this so I would maintain my connection with Spirit but of course I didn't understand that then. One day, I was feeling particularly sad so I asked a young boy who lived behind Gran Mc Cleese, I asked him to strangle me. I still remember his hands around my throat, squeezing it so tightly. Suddenly, I panicked and got him to stop, I can still remember that moment so clearly, I just wanted to sadness to stop.

It seems to have been an energy that raised its head every now and then. I just felt like I didn't belong here. An interesting pattern now that I look back on it. I expect many of you reading this would understand that feeling of not belonging, it is a common thing for us Starseeds.

Back to my travels after that slight deviation. The date was important to me.

We arrived in Rome, to another mail stop, I had three letters from Mum and one from my sister, deeply appreciated. I still remember the anxiety of waiting for my name to be read out for the mail, wow! Talk about waiting with bated breath, it was just so important hearing from home. Writing back was a bit challenging at times, trying to find Post Offices was my excuse I think. Just full on days, early mornings, late nights, the time just flew by. We visited the Vatican Museums, the Sistine Chapel and the statue of Romelus and Remus. Our Couch guide had this shirt of Romulus and Remus, with various alcoholic spirits coming from the wolf's teats then the last one was milk and it was being spat out! I found that quite funny. He also had another tee shirt, Fly United, with two Geese joined, he had an interesting sense of humour obviously.

We visited the Colosseum and I took a photo of a piece of original Roman road along the Apien Way. The Tivoli Fountain was quite impressive. We visited so many Churches and museums on this trip I was sick of circular staircases by the time I got home.

We visited the leaning Tower of Pizza and got a photo of us pretending to hold the tower up like the photo in our brochure! We climbed the Tower, very interesting experience indeed. Got a photo of the sculpture of David, such an amazing marble sculpture, extremely impressive indeed!

Venice was so impressive. The city is sinking and the Government we were told has been given a lot of money to save it but up till then nothing had been done about it! The Buses can only park at the beginning part as only foot traffic is allowed actually in Venice itself. The campsite we stayed at was called "Little Australia" Oh my goodness, the mosquitoes were so thick! There is a huge square with a magnificent church, Saint Marks Square I think it is called. I was very impressed with Venice I must admit.

I came to the conclusion Italians were very good at counting as from memory buying something small like biscuits were 200 Lire. I just couldn't wrap my head around how many Lire a car or a house would cost. We entered Salzburg where celebrations were in progress, there were some pretty amazing and colourful costumes. It was lovely watching the Folk Dancing and the procession. We saw the house where Sound of Music was filmed and Salisbury Castle.

München, Munich was our next port of call, the October Fest was in full swing, interesting experience indeed! We went out to Dachau, oh my goodness I felt the energy from like half an hour away from it, it was so thick! A vast room with pipes coming out from the walls, it was set up as a large shower but of course they were gassed instead! Really needed a chainsaw to cut through that atmosphere, it gives me chills even now, over forty years later. Back in München the Glockenspiel clock was very interesting to watch, every hour the act would go on for around 15 minutes. There were quite detailed segments of the clock doing various different things, very interesting. Next stop was Neuschwanstein in the Bavarian Alps. On one side of us we have a big clear lake, on the other side is the very impressive Neuschwanstein Castle which we visited. We then went through Germany, Austria, the tiny country of Liechtenstein and into Switzerland. We went up to the Jungfrau, the highest railway station in the world. The sky was bright blue and there was quite a glare from the snow. Pretty amazing to have built a railway station so high up in the snow of the mountain. The train must have had very powerful engines to get up there. I wonder if it went up there in the snow, I don't know.

Geneva was our next stop, got some photos of the bears in Bern. We did a tour of Paris by night and checked out all the regular sites including the Eiffel Tower which they referred to as the aweful tower.

Quite a magnificent view from up there however. Got to practice my French for the second time since High School. I was blown away by the amount of lanes of traffic around the Arch de Triumph, it was crazy! I must admit by the time we got to Notre Dame I was overflowing with Culture from all the art galleries and museums we had seen on the trip. It is a very impressive building indeed.

By the time I got back to London I was only staying there till 7pm the following night when I was departing on a 42 day tour through Spain, Portugal and Morocco. It was supposed to be Algeria and Tunisia as well but the bus broke down in the Sahara Desert on my 22nd birthday so we went back the way we came.

I spent months camping through these countries and my 22nd birthday was spent in the middle of the Sahara Desert waiting for our bus to get fixed! Finally at 10 p.m. that night we arrived at the Meninski Oasis! We were very good at putting our tents up by that time so doing it in the dark wasn't an issue! Waking up in the morning to that magnificent view and interesting smells was something I will never forget!

Doing these trips through all those countries it didn't take long for me to feel like I was playing with Monopoly money! We got very good at finding the right places to exchange our money, far away from the Tourist places. We would go into the local markets to buy our food, I got very good at talking with my hands, lol That has stayed with me ever since! As we entered each country we would be given basic phrases and a few words. We would also have the traditional dish of every country when we were there, frogs legs and escargot in France for example. In Spain they refused to tell us what we ate until after we had eaten it, they were bulls balls! Staying awake all night in Finland and being able to walk around the wooded campsite with ease as it was during their 6 months of daytime, was another awesome experience. Going into Russia when the KGB was a powerful force was such a restrictive energy. It was very thick and heavy, seeing old women dressed in black sweeping the streets with stick brooms blew my mind! We saw mass weddings as well; it was compulsory for them to go to war memorials. Everyone had to visit Lenin's Tomb, every 3 months I think from memory. We managed to go on a day when the queue was only short, it took us 3 hours to get through!

People lined up for everything in Russia. You couldn't tell from the outside of the shop whether it was a butcher or a baker! Mockba (Mocso) had the best vanilla ice-cream I have ever tasted, it was done between a couple of wafers, absolutely divine! I still have a bag of black and white photos I took on the trip. One was of the leaning Tower of Pisa where we were pretending to push the Tower back upright. The Little Mermaid in Copenhagen was much smaller than I thought it would be! I got Barcelona Belly real bad! We were in and out of Germany 7 times, on the last time we went back and asked for our passports to be stamped. In Turkey and Morocco the men were desperate to connect with a woman from Australia so they could marry you and come out here, I was so repulsed by this. I did meet a gentleman who was involved with the leather industry in Turkey, I went to dinner with him, was very lucky to get back to my Tour. When we were in Russia a few of us were chosen to go to a Russian home for dinner. They were the heads of companies, feeding us champagne and caviar and trying to tell us it was a typical Russian home! The trees along the sides of the road were still young and you could see into the fields and the villages. Oh man, you could smell the toilets a mile away, the up market ones had metal foot plates each side of the hole, you were expected to squat! That was a mind blowing experience, big time! Some of the others on the Tour brought jeans to be sold on the Black Market in Russia. The Guide we were given would stay up late talking to us, the KGB ended up taking her away and gave us another one, she was telling us too much Truth, and they didn't like it! We attended the Beer Fest, Octoberfest, in München. We visited many Art Galleries and Cathedrals, we walked up so many spiral staircases. We went to the top viewing platform of the Eiffel Tower (nick named the aweful tower).

CHAPTER THREE

More to explore

My second trip with Atrek Tours. You had to be under 30 years old to do these tours so turning 30 was really hard for me, my mother bless her, made me a 30 key in bread, it was so sweet of her and meant so much to me.

The first stop was Paris where once again, it was raining! We even had to take our tents down in the rain. The next day we crossed a mountain range where light snow was falling, it was so picturesque! We stayed in a hotel in Andora which was a real treat from camping for so long. Andora is definitely a place to go for Duty free in 1976. They speak French and Spanish and both currencies are used. If you use the Spanish currency things were cheaper. The scenery here reminded me of Lauterbrunnen. The road follows the stream through the valley, so beautiful. We visited a Monastery which contained the black Madonna and child. Spaniards have pilgrimages here. In Barcelona I was introduced to Sangria, oh boy, it gave me such a hangover. I was having such fun drinking it from the hide bag, I drink very rarely. The hangover the next morning was brutal and windy roads and I don't get on very well at the best of times, let alone with a hangover! Lesson learnt big time!

Checked out Madrid after being given a tour of it in the bus, it was time to do a wander and a closer inspection. I was fascinated that the roads radiated out in a circle. It was on the road to Toledo that my hangover hit me, I felt okay when I woke up, even had breakfast! We visited many Cathedrals and museums. I had a fascination for taking photos of unusually shaped buildings during both my trips, never had an interest in architecture before.

Our watches go back an hour once we enter Portugal. Got really good at understanding exchange rates after you go through a couple of countries. I was surprised to see Gum trees in Portugal. The whitewashed houses especially in the country really made quite an impression on me. The bus had its first breakdown just as we entered Spain from Portugal. It was an hour and a half ferry crossing to Morocco. It was another hour and a half at the border which was really good because it is not unusual to be there up to four hours. Such a treat to get our tents up while it was still light. We visit the King's Palace in Medina which is approx. 26 acres. Saw a Tannery, oh man, I still remember the smell and energy of that Tannery, it is not pleasant at all.

We leave Fez and head for Rabat for lunch and to get out visas for Tunisia. The Embassy was closed so we had to stay the night. Went back at midday to pick up our visas after arriving at the Embassy at 8.30 a.m. We bypass Casablanca on our way to Marrakesh. The ground was so hard us girls slept in the cook tent. We walk around the Medena, the main square. I went for a carriage ride for an hour around Marrakesh and took a heap of photos. Going for a ride on a donkey was an interesting experience, the donkey parking area we saw some very interesting activity to say the least, doing what comes naturally but hung like a donkey certainly took on a whole new meaning for me, I was chuckling to myself, I couldn't believe the size. It would touch the ground, I wonder if they ever got blisters there?

On my birthday I see the sunrise as it went from red to golden orange. I feel very alone and find myself missing Rudy badly, hoping we can get back together again, it doesn't happen! My time with him is over and I am in for some massive lessons over the next 17 years of my life. I admit, on a Soul level I asked for them so I could become visible to myself but to say they made my life a living hell is an understatement!

As we leave the hotel, our guide tells us, two and a half hours to Meninski Oasis at the most! About ten kilometres out from the closest town to the hotel the back axle of our bus breaks! I remember thinking to myself," This is one birthday you will never forget! "Sitting on that red hot sand, not knowing how long we were going to be there, wondering when we would be able to have some water to drink, curious as to how we were going to continue our trip even. I remember the time passed very slowly in that hot desert sun. We had to get a truck to tow the bus. Playmates, another bus company arrives and they pile us and all our gear onto their bus. We arrive at Meninski Oasis in the dark. At tea they sang Happy Birthday to me, three bottles of Champagne were consumed. It ended up being a pretty good day, full of drama and stress but it ended well. There were some very interesting smells there. What a sight we woke up to, they have a pretty good set up with a freshwater pool with fish, it is a flow through pool. It was wonderful lazing around all day sunbaking and swimming. The Courier takes some underwater film of us. I meet a really nice guy from Playmates who gave me a precious birthday present which was gratefully accepted. How interesting, he comes from Elsternwick in Tramville, you wouldn't believe who you can meet in the middle of the Sahara Desert. I was living in Elsternwick when I had my 21st birthday! What a massive contrast this one was!

I went into the nearest village with people from the Contiki Tour in the morning and spend the afternoon lazing about again. The flies are pretty bad here and they have huge ants as well. One of the guys pushes me into the pool, all part of the fun. We were stuck at the Oasis for four full days getting news on the fifth day we would be leaving around noon so there was a mad rush to get everything packed. Three cheers arose when the bus appears on the scene. The next day we get about fifty kilometres from Figuig, our first desert stop, we discovered that either water or diesel was leaking into the oil which meant that the engine could seize any time so we had to limp back to London.

That was the straw that broke the camel's back! So appropriate when you are in the middle of the Sahara, pardon the pun! In fact, the bus has trouble in starting after our first loo stop so we missed out on Algeria and Tunisia. We come through the Atlas mountains where it has been snowing, some of us decide we want to have a snow fight. The road side is fairly slippery and on a fairly steep slope. As a result we end up in a ditch at a ten degree slope although it certainly felt much more! We were stuck there until a bus full of Burbas gave us a hand to push her out! The Courier says, "no more stops". Just as Fez comes into sight our headlights die on us so we spent three quarters of an hour fixing them. We have tea at a cafe then drive all night to get to the ferry. We get to the boarder at 4am.

After all that rushing, we discover the ferry leaves at 3.30pm, not 10am, as a result we have a little time to kill on our hands unexpectedly.

Our next overnight stop had top class facilities, the showers were hot and free and stayed hot for ages! The things we take for granted. We mixed a lot with the Contiki passengers making more friends. There was a fog lying over Grenada as we leave. It looked really strange as we climbed the mountains, all over the valley was this huge cloud like you would see out from a plane window. It was nice and sunny on the other side of the range. We ended up arriving in Alicanti not long after Contiki, we had had just finished putting up their tents. We had left Grenada about two hours after they had.

The next day it was a long drive to Barcelona, arriving after dark. Checked out Barcelona the next day, we found a Hypermarket, never came across one before. The next day we eventually leave half an hour late after fond farewells. We spend about one and a half hours at the French boarder while the bus got thoroughly searched. We drive through to Carciconne, the road sort of island hopped like it did when we were coming into Copenhagen. We had lunch at Arles. The camp at Antibes was quite close to the sea. We could see snow-capped mountains in the distance. We visited the perfume factory and I bought some Jasmine perfume. Jasmine incense holds a lot of memories for me as that is what my daughter's father bought for me for my 17th birthday.

From here we headed for Monaco and to the Monte Carlo Casino.

When we arrived we went looking for the Police station as we were told we could get a passport stamp of Monaco there but the information we received was incorrect.

We leave Antibes at 5.30 a.m. and meet up with the other Atrek bus. The road seems to get a bit rough, after a while we can smell smoke! We have a puncture on our inside right tyre! We arrive in Paris at 9pm, it is raining but we are able to stay in a hotel. I am on the 5ᵗʰ floor and there is even a little balcony. I feel so sorry for the others in the camp site, they would have got saturated sadly. I am able to have a hot shower and wash my hair and some clothes, gee it felt so good! We do the sights of Paris and are dropped off at the Louvre. The next day I walk down the Arc de Triumph to see the parade for the 11. 11.11. There is a huge French flag flying under the Arch. I walked both sides of the Champs-Élysées. I enjoyed eating in the Latin Quarter. After dinner we headed off to where the artists work at the top of the hill, the red line district is at the bottom of the hill. Quite the colourful place indeed. Next port of call was the Eiffel Tower and the fountains are actually playing, that was a pleasant surprise indeed. The Arc de Triomphe was our next destination, there were lights behind the large flag which shone about halfway down the Champs-Élysées. Under the Arc de Triomphe the military were holding the flags of many different countries. Those lights left a huge impression on my mind. What a farewell from Paris.

Of all my travels I think the French and Italian drivers were the craziest. We arrive at Calais at 4 p.m. I am amazed at how large it is, didn't really get to appreciate it on the way over.

After I spent some time back in London I decided to go back to the Netherlands. I had organised a two-day stay in Amsterdam and an eight-day stay in a bed and breakfast in the town where Rudy was born, Beverwijk. I had done adult Dutch classes before I left Tramville, I was pleased when the locals thought I was also Dutch, blonde hair in plaits and blue eyes, well it was a good disguise, I could understand far more than I could speak. Rudy's parents would speak Dutch at home and ask me how much I understood.

I left London at 9.40 a.m. for Amsterdam. I have a second class train ticket and a first class ticket on the boat. On the way over I met a "Rudy" type guy. It was not until we were docking that I spoke to him as I had a feeling he wasn't English. I was right, he was from Hamburg, West Germany, his name was Alwin. Before we went through Customs, we exchanged addresses. A goodbye kiss was given before we parted.

There was a very thick fog on the way over and the boat was quite late getting in. It was after 10 pm by the time I arrived in Amsterdam. I had a map of Amsterdam and tried to walk to the Hotel but got lost so I hired a taxi who also got lost! Not good!

Finally around 11pm I eventually arrived at the Hotel. After the formalities were completed I was escorted up three flights of very steep, narrow stairs to my little room. I was rather glad of the comfy bed with sheets even, such a treat after using sleeping bags for so long! It was still quite a novelty even after staying in the Hotel in Paris I arrive for breakfast at 9.30am to this neat homely dining room. I am greeted in English," Good morning, sleep well?". Breakfast consisted of a boiled egg, four pieces of bread, jam, meat and cheese with a glass of hot chocolate. Oh boy, those stairs, you wouldn't want to be sleep walking anywhere near them, so dangerous for those of us who were not use to such narrow steps! Going up and down them would keep you very fit for sure, and I am only 22 years old and they are scaring me! I spent the day becoming familiar with Amsterdam. I am quite close to the Reichs museum, the post office is across the road from it.

On one of my many departures from the hotel I overheard one of the officials saying a very naughty Dutch word as he made a mistake. My eyes must have popped out of my head at which he was greatly surprised I had understood what he had said so he explained and apologised. Funny how when you are learning a new language, the swear words are often learnt very quickly, that is what happens when your partner is Dutch anyway!. I offered another version of what he said that doesn't mean anything, he was quite amused!

I should look like pineapple yoghurt by now I have eaten so much of it. The food you are drawn to eating when you are on a shoe string budget. The first time I was in the Netherlands, I actually bought a round block of Edam cheese so cheese and crackers were another one of my staple diets. The next day breakfast was the same as yesterday. I asked him to keep my fifteen guilders key deposit for when I returned from Beverwijk. I waved them farewell as I headed for the station. It is 4.25 guilders for a single ticket. I just missed a train so needed to wait half an hour for the next one., I was very grateful that they ran regularly. We passed through a very long tunnel just before we arrived in Beverwijk. I arrived at midday but had to wait till two pm so I could book a hotel. Once again I headed for the main street to check out the little village. I find a Dutch for Travellers book and a map of Beverwijk, it helped to kill the time. I finally connect with my room and discover the hospital is just across the road from where I am staying. Oh boy, that brought up a lot of emotion, I had come here because this is where Rudy was born. I dug deep and found the courage to ask about the old hospital. It had been knocked down, the new hospital was built on the same site about three years beforehand. I pay the TV room a visit and discover I am the only female. I am able to watch the Mary Tyler Moore show, in English!

The next day I take myself downtown and buy a few items, a ring took my interest, very emotional, I really miss Rudy. I take myself on a guided tour taking heaps of photos as I go.

The Dutch display marzipan goodies in the shop windows, they also do chocolate letters so I bought a R to bring home with me. It is December and they are getting ready for Sinta Klaus which is a black man, much to my surprise. I saw the procession through town later on, very impressed. On the way back to the Hotel I came across a bookstore and decided to check it out. I came across a Lilliput woordenbook, it is so small (Nederlands / Engles), you need a magnifying glass to read it! It is a whole two inches by one and a half inches, by half an inch so you can understand why a magnifying glass would be so badly needed! It was so tiny and cute, I couldn't resist buying it. In fact I still have it forty two years later!.

The next day I am off on further adventures and I met up with the Sinta Klaus parade, I was totally fascinated by how different it was to our Santa. Sinta Klaus's birthday is celebrated on the sixth December I was told.

That night I check out the local phone book and find one of Rudy's relatives still live there. Yes, I checked out the address but was too afraid to knock on the door and introduce myself. When I got back to Tramville his mother told me I should have knocked on the door and introduced myself, oh well. Nice to know I would have had his mum's approval to be so bold. The next day, around seven pm I spotted Rudy's twin, just goes to show how similar family members can be, it really blew my mind. It was like he had never left there. I was amazed how people would greet me in Dutch, not realising I was Australian, I really fitted in there very well.

It was nearly time to come back to Tramville so the next day I made my way back to Amsterdam, stayed the night then headed back to London. I made the trip because I was running away from Rudy and the hurt and pain of our relationship ending. Looking back now I am really pleased I did that trip when I did before I had children. It was such an amazing experience and I would thoroughly recommend to others, travel before you settle down and have a family. Of course you can travel with children but it is easier and cheaper to do it on your own!

CHAPTER FOUR

Meeting the narcissist

When I got back to the hospital I was working at, a new porter had started work. I felt like a failure because I hadn't got married and I was desperate to do so. When he started paying me attention I was so excited. I totally understand the emptiness, the loneliness, the sheer and utter desperation to have someone in your life to keep you company. The fear of being on your own and, for me, ending up a lonely old spinster, was a totally horrifying thought! I needed someone in my life to make me feel whole and complete. Girls I went to school with were getting married and settling down with families. Having children was also important to me, pretty hard to do without a partner, preferably one who wanted to marry you first.

The Matron bless her, was really supportive of me after the breakup of my relationship with Rudy and the D and C, I had in order for him to stay in my life. Depression had kicked in due to out of balance hormones and yes I was suicidal. Rudy took me to the hospital. After he dropped me off I never saw him again. The Matron realised the new porter was a Narcissist, so forbid me to be with him. I left, and we moved in together! My fear of being alone was so powerful, I was willing to lose my job in order to be with someone. The Matron told me I shouldn't be in a relationship as she knew about my break up with Rudy and my D and C. There I go again, so desperate to have someone in my life. I did as Rudy asked and got rid of the child, he promised to stay with me if I did that! Fear and loneliness have you do some pretty crazy things. We got engaged and we were going to get married on Valentine's Day the next year. We had a massive argument one day and to make it up to me he told me we would get married as soon as possible. I had all these bells go off in my head, I thought they were Wedding bells, but NO, they were alarm bells! If this ever happens to you, RUN!!!

We got married three months after meeting each other. He had his mother, brother and sister trained to do and say what he wanted them to. On his 19th birthday he had them pretend it was his 21st birthday. Remember, I was 22 at this time, that was a huge age gap which is why he pretended he was turning 21. His father had died when he was 15 and he was the eldest child. His mother was an alcoholic, his father was a control freak. For years I tried to work out if his mother drank because his father was a control freak or his father was a control freak because his mother drank.

Several decades later I learn about Empathic Rescuers and Victims who can also be Narcissists.

As Rescuers we have such a massive need to be needed we are experts at being invisible to ourselves, always putting everyone else before us. This happens because way back in our childhood, we took on board the belief pattern that we did not deserve which is why we only allow ourselves to GIVE! We find receiving extremely hard to do, massively challenging even, because guilt tends to haunt us!

Feeling incomplete on our own, or as I call it, being half an apple, needing someone else to make us feel whole and complete, opens the door to another half apple, a Victim or far worse, a Narcissist to come into our lives. They "Love Bomb" us for three or four months then start criticising us for the very things they praised us for or liked about us. This leaves us desperately trying to work out what we did wrong and trying to "fix it". Oh boy, do we get sucked in! It is like going down a greased slide, you cannot stop until you hit rock bottom.

Sadly many Empaths have a parent who is a Narcissist so to them, that crazy abusive behaviour is "normal". I have a beautiful friend who had a Narc mother, ended up married to another Narc for forty years, had a rebound relationship with another Narc, before we became friends. I did meet him three years ago but he was still in the rebound relationship then. Him and I are looking at co writing a book about our journeys with Narcissists to help other Empaths, both male and female.

As a 22 year old, I had no idea about this! All I knew was that I believed there was something wrong with me because I failed to get married after a two year engagement. I bet some of you have felt like failures because your relationships failed to work out. For many of us, Mills and Boone Romantic novels of tender loving care and support as love, are pure fantasy.

We need to understand, our "Love Equation" is formed during the first seven years of our lives.

Abandonment on an emotional or physical level. A single parent family, a parent who is a workaholic or being unable to emotionally communicate translates into us bringing partners into our life who love us by Abandoning us! When our parents fight, it means chaos becomes our Love Equation, and we repeat these patterns in our own relationships. We can heal and change our patterns. It is called doing our Inner Child Work.

There is also a beautiful lady by the name of MELANIE TONIA EVANS. She has written a book called, "You can thrive after Narcissistic Abuse." She has developed a system for recovering from Toxic Relationships. She has You Tube Videos, a Blog and offers a Course to assist with your Healing Journey. You can find her on Face Book also. If you are ready to begin your Healing Journey, I strongly suggest you check her out. She nearly died herself from Narcissistic abuse so she really knows what she is talking about! She has been recognised for her work by other professionals for the results she obtains for her clients.

Meanwhile, back to my journey with the Narcissist, I discovered very early on, there are two faces of a Narcissist. A sweet innocent, butter wouldn't melt in his mouth side which he showed the public. Behind closed doors however the cruel, nasty side of him came out.

Nobody believes you when you tell them what the Narcissist is doing because of the mask they wear in public. Gas Lighting is one of their favourite tools, they want to make you think you are crazy. They constantly lie and whatever they blame you for doing, is exactly what they are doing! He had many affairs after we got divorced, and probably before if the truth is told. Talk about Abandonment being played out! I" walked on eggshells" for seventeen years, never knowing what was going to upset him next. Believe me, stress like that is very bad for your health, mental, emotional and physical. By the way, you CANNOT EVER FIX A NARCISSIST! Forget trying harder to please then, they thrive on your misery!

I found out later on he would bash his mother up if she got stuck in the pub and forget to pick his siblings up from school. Didn't take him long to start bashing me up as well after we got married and there began seventeen years of hell, walking on eggshells, never knowing what was going to upset him next and yes, he was an alcoholic as well. Champagne Cocktails really brought the monster out in him He would drive the car with me and our son in it when he couldn't even walk a straight line! He would swerve over the road, bang on the steering wheel, break suddenly or accelerate where it was inappropriate, yes, my heart was in my mouth whenever I got in the car with him. I lost count of how many minced mouths I experienced, he would tell his family my wisdom teeth were playing up badly. I was lucky that my sister and my parents woke up to what he was doing. I am very grateful to my sister, she would come and see me refusing to allow him to cut her out of my life. Right at the beginning of my relationship with him my sister, who was living in Adelaide at the time, invited me to spend some time with her. I know that if it had been a month later into our relationship, he would have prevented me from going.

My sister was very good at making wrap around maxi skirts so she helped me make one when I was over there with her. It was a light blue colour with small flowers on it. I had a wonderful time with her.

Once the Narcissist got himself firmly entrenched into my life my life just went downhill once the "Love Bombing" period was over. My mother would know the Latin name for various plants, my sister was the same. She has loved doing bush walks since our parents bought her a little yellow mini minor. It gave her freedom and she just loves driving, quite the cruiser, my daughter is the same. Myself on the other hand, find it very challenging to drive anywhere for over two hours, I prefer to just potter about in my local area.

It was amazing he never killed us in the car. Obviously Spirit was keeping us safe even back then when I never knew about my Sky Family. One day we were turning right and a car hit us from behind forcing us into an oncoming car which also hit us. I ended up in hospital and lost the ability to walk for a while, I was still pregnant at that stage. When my parents came to visit me in the hospital my mother realised he had been abusing me and that he was a Narcissist which I didn't understand at that time.

I was just so grateful to have had been able to get married. We got married on the twenty sixth of March, a whole three months after we met, I must have been crazy as well as desperate!

I would NEVER advise anyone to get married after only three months of meeting someone! I forgot to tell you, if your partner tells you within the first few days they are madly in love with you, they are a Narcissist! RUN!!!

I will slightly digress here, we were supposed to get married in the Botanical gardens but apparently you needed a permit which we didn't have so we ended up getting married at the War Memorial. Oh boy, that symbolised our marriage perfectly! One long war! On our wedding night, he went out with his mates and left me alone in the motel room. He blocked me from my friends and my family and basically isolated me, so he could abuse me without anyone interfering because his mother was in no fit state to stand up for me. She was an alcoholic and Michael had been physically and emotionally abusing her since his father died when he was 15. I finally worked out that it was his father that was the Narcissist.

Michael loved the idea of the power and control having people fear him, really made his day! He regularly bashed up his brother who was really nice to me. His brother ended up moving to Perth to get away from him, right across the other coast of Australia! Did I mention Narcissists are major control freaks, oh yes, they must have everything their way! They have no compassion and they are always right! They are the bullies of society, of course we cannot leave out the Psychopaths and the Sociopaths. I wish we could place these people in the Fema Camps they have created for the rest of us!

CHAPTER FIVE

We need to remember, we are the role models for our children, as our parents were our Role Models! What we need to remember however is our parents raised us to the best of their ability as we raised our own children. If we can look at how our parents were raised, then we have a better understanding of why they raised us the way they did! Some of us are "chain breakers" and we break the patterns of our parents with our own children. Sadly some people go totally opposite of what they grew up with so they may have grown up with very strict boundaries, they may give their children absolutely no boundaries. A middle road is the best, it is all about balance. Children need boundaries so they can learn the consequences of their behaviour and right from wrong. Normal people understand we are not perfect and we make mistakes, well okay, let us put that another way, we learn the lessons that on a Soul level, we set up for ourselves.

Society says our parents "Love" us, sadly that "love" is not always tender loving care and support. It is often abandonment as in the case of single parent families, or when a parent is a workaholic or even when parents don't know how to emotionally communicate!. We cannot pass anything onto our children that we don't know how to do ourselves so it becomes a generational pattern. The same goes for abuse, be it physical or emotional!

I grew up with my father using the strap and electric cord to discipline us, he had a horse whip used on him! I only ever used my hand to discipline my children, that way it hurt me as well. Many people do not understand how damaging emotional abuse is. The sub conscious find fails to differentiate between Truth and a Lie. Whatever we are told over and over becomes a reality in our lives as the sub conscious just obeys what we keep telling it. The good news with this is that we are the ones in charge of our thought patterns so WE CAN CHANGE THEM! Okay, so our reality will not change overnight unfortunately, we need to remember the negative beliefs have been with us all our lives, often several decades before we learn to change them. Stress, anxiety, panic attacks are common with us Empathic Rescuers when we are in a relationship with a Narcissist. It is even worse when one of our parents is a Narcissist! Our minds are jam packed with negative thought patterns so it is going to take many months of handwriting one page every day, the new thought pattern that you wish to create. When you are writing out the new thought pattern for the new reality you wish to experience, you MUST write in the PRESENT TENSE! Using "will" pushes things off into the future and as we all know, the future NEVER ARRIVES!

We cannot heal anything we are not aware of so the first step is to become aware of what beliefs / thought patterns we are holding onto. I have found that by sitting quietly and observing our thought patterns as they come to the surface, without judgement! Take a note of them any way you feel comfortable doing it, just so you are aware of what you are dealing with, what is sabotaging you!

What I suggest you do next is to turn these negative belief patterns around to positive thoughts in the PRESENT TENSE! Using "will" just pushes things away into the future and I am sure you want to bring this new reality into your present not your future!

Now there is no point handwriting your positive new belief that you want to create for a week and when it doesn't manifest, throw your hands up in the air declaring it doesn't work! You must allow the new thought pattern / belief pattern, to work its way through the massive thickness of decades of negative thoughts, before it can manifest into your reality! Patience is a very challenging lesson to learn. Remember, most of these thoughts/beliefs have been reinforced by others since you were a child! Learning to be nice to ourselves is very challenging due to the belief that we don't deserve.

The other part of this exercise is the practical where you catch yourself doing NICE things for yourself! Mind you, us Rescuers have an A+ in giving and a Z- in receiving as our belief pattern says that we don't deserve so we do invisibility to ourselves really well! It can take us many decades for us to learn to be visible to ourselves! An activity I suggest to my clients is to get an exercise book and call this your Nurturing book. Of course those of you with technology devices may like to go into the Notes section or journal, you can tell I am an IT Dinosaur. Every time you do something nice for yourself, it doesn't even have to cost money, just time for yourself. I know this is massively challenging for a lot of you who run around like headless chooks after people who are never there for you. I have a magic word for you to learn, it is called NO! To be used liberally on people who are never there for you! Forget the excuses and reasons, Victims are really good at working their way around them, simply, NO it is not convenient! End of story!

Write down the date, what it was that you did and give yourself a massive tick! Remember when you were at Primary school and you got a maths sum right, how good that tick made you feel? Well, doing this is like becoming a parent / teacher to your Inner Child, giving them constant rewards and encouraging them to receive!

In the first month you may only do one thing as the invisibility factor is rather massive, come the second month you may do two things. The more you do it the easier it gets. I can assure you, this will be very challenging for you to do due to our belief pattern that tells us that we don't deserve!

Start with small things, listening to music, allowing yourself to rest for half an hour when you are feeling tired, spending time in nature such as bush walking or going to the beach, a lake or river. Even spending time in the garden is excellent. Some people are very creative, cooking, sewing, knitting, crocheting, drawing, painting, writing etc. Give yourself half an hour every day of "do not disturb time", where you are free to nurture yourself in whatever way you fancy. You will feel so much better and recharged after doing something nice for yourself.

Many of us have bad habits that are not very good for our health, maybe at some stage we could honour ourselves and decide to stop doing those destructive activities so our health can improve. Thankfully I don't drink or smoke, giving up those things are so extremely challenging so my congratulations to all of those of you who have reduced or stopped these activities. You don't have to do it on your own, there are professionals and things like Nicotine patches, even Hypnotherapy can be of assistance.

For me it is food, needing to eat healthier, I have an addiction to carbohydrates. It doesn't help that I have lunch with a girlfriend every Wednesday and part of our pattern is having a naughty desert with our lunch.

Another nurturing thing you can do for yourself is to reduce your weight which there is a lot of support professionally to assist you to do this. When we have been emotionally / physically abused, our body creates a "Cubby House" to feel safe. We will never keep our weight off if we don't deal with the issues our body is protecting us from. Mind you I understand genetic disposition may also play a part so doing exercise may be helpful if we just sit around all day with our job.

Once again, Emotional Healing is not something we can complete in a weekend unfortunately, remember, many of us have been emotionally damaged for decades! Of course if you begin doing your Emotional Healing work as a teenager, it is not going to take you as long to do as those of us in our sixties!

Watching what foods we eat, watching the portions we give ourselves, is a very obvious way to lose weight. I have released a massive amount of weight by identifying through Kinesiology my optimum eating time which is from 5pm to 10pm, totally contrary to what doctors and Nutritionists tell you.

We are all individuals and sometimes our bodies operate better not having three main meals a day. My girlfriend has six small meals during the day.

I have type one, generalised Lymphodoema which means my whole body holds extra fluid not just a single limb. When I was coming back from Couldville in 2012 the plane was late leaving Phoenix. I had half an hour before the plane left for Brisbane, it takes an hour for the luggage to come across and you were not allowed on the plane without your luggage so I couldn't get another plane till the next afternoon. Now in order for the swelling in my body to go down, putting my feet up just doesn't help. I need to lay down flat! By the time I got into Sydney I looked like the Michelin Man! I was so blown up it was challenging to bend because I had nowhere to actually lay down flat. I did find a lounge but the seat didn't lay down flat. By the time I got back to Brisbane my daughter was scared to touch me fearing I would burst like a balloon. I felt like I could also, it was scary! From memory it took many hours of laying down before I could bend comfortably again. I do find that when I have lunch my weight tends to pile back on again much to my sheer frustration.

Many of us are very hard on ourselves, perfectionists even, and we give ourselves a very hard time when we make a mistake or slip up when we are attempting to stop smoking, drinking or reduce the amount of our weight. That is when we then tend to go right off the rails and end up doing a bender smoking, drinking or eating extra.

We need to be gentle with ourselves, in my world I see this as a School of Life and if we were perfect we wouldn't need to be here in the first place. We cannot change our behaviour if we are unaware of what we are doing so when we catch ourselves "slipping up" for whatever reason, only then we can do something to change our behaviour so congratulate yourself on becoming aware of what you were doing. That is the only time you can do something different, when you have the awareness and of course the willingness to do something different! When we are making positive changes in our lives it sometimes feels like we are taking three steps forwards and two steps backwards and often times we get extremely frustrated with this behaviour of ours! What we often fail to realise we have still taken one step forward with our progress, when we take two steps back it gives us the opportunity to review what we are doing.

Sometimes we need to tweak what we are doing and try a new method or pathway, that is fine! There are many pathways which lead us to the end result we are desiring! Occasionally there is a time constraint but often there isn't. One of my favourite sayings is "Everything happens in Divine Timing, not ours!" Just be gentle with yourselves! We cannot change anything we are not aware of, just remember that! Some of these patterns we have, have been with us for decades, give yourself a break and never mind which bone those of you who are really cheeky! Allow yourself to take baby steps, after all, what is the best way to metaphorically eat an elephant / solve a problem, ? To break it down into bite sized pieces! When it is a large task, break it down into smaller manageable tasks or pieces. Give it a go, it may stop you from going into overwhelm of having panic attacks.

Dealing with stress / panic attacks I would suggest stopping and taking several slow deep breaths, blowing into a paper bag when you are hyperventilating, I also find Bach Flower Rescue Remedy has been extremely beneficial. Some teas like Camomile can be used to relax you as well to assist you to sleep. Experiment see what suits you. Consult a Counsellor, Hypnotherapist, Alternative Therapist or doctor if you need further assistance in keeping you calm and relaxed. It is amazing how letting go of the need to fix other people can reduce your stress level! After all, the only adults behaviour you have any control over is YOUR OWN! I know this is extremely challenging to do when you are a Rescuer with a deep need to be needed and a massive invisibility to yourself issue to deal with due to a low self-esteem.

As we are Healing, we really need to address Emotional and Mental causes as well as Physical causes. In my world I look at Soul Contracts, we don't remember what Soul Contracts we make before we get here so personally I have found Energy Healing work invaluable as it deals with not only this Life time but Past Lives as well. Some people find Reiki, Kinesiology, Acupuncture, and Acupressure extremely valuable resources in their Healing Journeys as well. Different strokes for different folks as the saying goes!

Seeing a Counsellor or someone with more qualifications like a

Psychologist or a Psychiatrist may be necessary due to the intensity of the Emotional and physical damage experienced.

One of the biggest issues us Empathic Rescuers have is learning to ask for help and to receive it because we are the Givers and basically totally invisible to ourselves. Our belief we took on board as a child which we interpreted as "We don't deserve" is a massive blockage for us moving forward.

Sometimes we will half do things for ourselves such as buying the Rescue Remedy to calm us down and release the anxiety we carry, but then we never end up taking it! News Flash friends, it doesn't work by osmosis, we have to actually take it, carrying it around in our bags is not going to help us at all

Using Crystals to ground us and keep us calm is an excellent tool I have found. Crystals such as Tigers Eye, Tourmaline and Smoky Quartz are very good for repelling Psychic attack, in other words, people sending you angry, negative thought forms.

Essential Oils such as Lavender can have a very calming effect. Please feel free to investigate which oils you feel would benefit you further! What works for one person may not suit another one so this is a very individual journey I highly recommend for you to take! Some people find Incense very calming and relaxing.

White sage can be used for smudging and clearing out negative energies as well. This is a very common practice that the Native Americans use, I love it! You need to fan the smoke of the sage into all the corners as that is where the energy tends to get stuck and hide! I burn my Sage in a Paua shell. You can also use a clay pot.

We need to remember, thought creates reality which has been proven scientifically, so "stinking thinking" can create quite a nasty reality for you! The good thing is when it comes to thoughts, this is something you actually DO HAVE CONTROL OVER! The frustrating part is understanding that when you change your negative thought to a positive one it does not instantly change your reality! You have been holding onto these negative thoughts, in many cases since you were a child, so you will need to write one page every day of the new reality you wish to experience until it manifests into your reality! Be patient, it may take many months for this to happen, keeping in mind, you have been holding onto the negative thoughts for decades in many cases, a few months is a relatively short time! Patience is an extremely challenging lesson for many of us!

May I suggest a good affirmation to use would be, I now have Peace and Harmony within me and around me, thank you! Now I can hear many of you say, but all I have is chaos and drama. We need to keep in mind that the sub conscious mind fails to differentiate between truth and a lie and creates whatever we keep telling it. Many people use "will" when they are setting their intentions however "will" pushes things off into the future and the future never arrives! Very frustrating I know which is why we need to use the present tense when we are doing this work to bring what we want into the here and now!

When we live in an "Attitude of Gratitude" that expands the energy of what we are asking for! Make a habit of writing down five things you are grateful for every day! If you cannot think of anything be thankful you are breathing and you can read so you can learn and grow. Hearing and sight are good.

CHAPTER SIX

Please, all you Empaths and Rescuers, if a partner puts you up on a pedestal, RUN!!!

If they are telling you how madly and passionately they are in love with you within the first day or so of meeting you, understand this is called "Love Bombing". When you are feeling desperately alone you tend to fall for this trick of the Narcissist, "Hook, line and sinker!" Needing someone else to make us feel whole and complete is what opens the door wide to a Narcissist!

Mind you, women can be Narcissists also. Society tends to "Look down its nose" at the men that are abused by women. Most of society expect men to be rough and tough and expect men to stand up for themselves. Unless you are an Empath, you cannot possibly understand how challenging it is to deal with all the energies you come across out in the public, let alone dealing with family and friends.

There are several tools an Empath can use to protect themselves, crystals, meditations and grounding are some of them. Please do your own research to find something that benefits you.

These beautiful soft, caring, compassionate men need all the help and support they can get! I have been with three of them in my life after I had escaped from my Narcissist. I must admit I was shocked when my first male Empath told me his wife had abused him, I had never heard about that before and I was forty at the time!

Society has come to terms with men abusing women but tend

to turn a blind eye when it is the other way around sadly. I must admit I am relieved Society no longer accepts Domestic Violence as acceptable behaviour.

Narcissists have been known to kill their Empathic / Rescuer partners when their physical abuse gets so bad.

Firstly I found the arguments and verbal abuse began after the "honeymoon period" of Love Bombing ended. This is known as Gas Lighting where the Narcissist tries to make you believe you are crazy! The next phase I experienced was "minced mouths", he would tell his mother that my wisdom teeth were playing up. The next stage he would knock me out. He hospitalised me a couple of times as well.

I was threatened with, "If you try to leave me I will find you and kill you!" Needless to say, I was extremely terrified to say the least! I was desperate to do anything to appease him so I wouldn't get abused. Talk about feeling trapped in an invisible cage. People asked me why I just didn't leave. The abject fear of being hunted down and killed, especially when you have children with the Narcissist, makes you stay. You convince yourself you can" fix" them! Nothing could be further from the truth! NARCISSISTS ARE UNFIXABLE! They like the power and control they have over you. They are MAJOR CONTROL FREAKS!

There was a game he would play with his sister where he would stand behind her and tell her to fall backwards and he would catch her. Every now and then he would step away and let her fall onto the floor. He thought it was hilarious, I was horrified! This was very early on in our relationship, I just thought it was very mean of him to do that to his sister! When his brother began being kind to me, he must have found out and use to bash him up badly. I was horrified when I discovered that was happening. After a while I was wondering why I never saw his younger brother. His sister informed me he had moved to Perth for work. I knew it was to escape from his abusive brother.

I never thought he would be abusing me far worse than that, I was desperate to be in a relationship. I just believed you had to accept the bad with the good and in a perfect world the good would far outweigh the bad. In the end, I felt a bit like a frog jumping from lily pad to lily pad trying to ignore all the hurt and pain in between the good times on the lily pads.

A Narcissist and will make your life a living hell. As soon as you are comfortable on that pedestal, they will start tearing you down and NOTHING you do will be good enough! Even things they praised you for before will not be good enough and you will be left scratching your head wondering what you did wrong. We bring them into our lives because we feel lonely and incomplete. On a Soul level, the role we ask them to play is to bring us to "crash and burn". To create so much intense pain within us that we actually become visible to ourselves, something us Rescuers have no idea how to do, because our core belief tends to run along the line of," I don't deserve".

Until we reach this point of intense pain, which will take longer for those of you who have grown up with a Narcissistic parent, due to you believing this abusive behaviour is "normal". We cannot begin our emotional healing journey. Doing our Inner Child work and becoming a parent to ourselves!

What we need to remember, for those of you with raised clubs figuratively speaking, who judge yourselves so harshly, is that NOTHING happens until the time is right! It is all about Divine Timing!

Who encouraged you to be the best you could possibly be by saying," Not good enough, do it again?" Where they left off, you then take over and are much harsher on yourself once you are an adult, perfectionists perhaps. You lead an extremely stressed life because of this tendency.

I spent the next 17 years attempting to escape him, three times I left, twice he found me again! I was a nervous wreck looking over my shoulder all the time afraid of bumping into someone or knows you who may tell him where they saw you, or worse still bumping into him.

The last time I saw him was Saint Patricks Day in Chadstone shopping Centre. We were in Target and he was up at the counter being served. He had this tendency of putting on this false Irish accent on when he was in public. He never used it at home or even when he was with his mother. I was with my daughter who was no longer the skinny young girl that he use to know. She was 16 and had put some weight on and had dyed her hair red. Apparently he asked my son who she was and was shocked at her transformation. Anyway, every time he opened his mouth and this false Irish accent fell out my daughter and I just burst out laughing! He was trying to chat up the young girl behind the counter. Tears were falling down my face I was laughing so much! What a massive turnaround from being absolutely terrified of him.

He actually came through in Evidence of Survival at Church a couple of months ago. I sent him away, I didn't want anything to do with him. A couple of weeks later he came through with Rob Lomax from England, on FB. I knew he had come for closure, for forgiveness. After all, he was just playing a role I had asked him to play so I could learn the lesson of becoming visible to myself. My parents came through first, they knew I would not accept him if he came on his own. Of course I was dealing with his Higher Self, so I was able to forgive him so we could both heal.

Talking about forgiveness, when we don't forgive someone it doesn't affect them at all but it surely destroys our mental, emotional and even physical health. So we forgive FOR OUR SAKE! It has nothing to do with them. It was a Soul Contract and they were just playing the role, we asked them to play before we incarnated.

You find yourself walking on eggshells, never knowing what they will get upset about next or blame you for. It is totally Soul destroying but eventually you come to a space of "What about me?" It normally takes many years to reach this point of straw breaking the camel's back so the saying goes.

This is a massive breakthrough because us Rescuers are extremely good at being invisible to ourselves! Going through crash and burn, I call it, being in maximum pain, is the only way we seem to achieve visibility of ourselves! Only then can we begin our Emotional Healing journey, and change our Love Equation from abandonment, and chaos to tender loving care and support. This is how we become the parent to our own Inner Child! To be able to look in the mirror and tell your seven year old child that you love them and that you will never leave them again and apologise to them. Allow this very emotionally damaged child to come out and play. Bring joy into their heart and a smile to their face. This can be through drawing, painting, cutting and pasting, going to the playground even and having a swing! Spending time in nature, playing with your pets, making things with blocks / Lego, make your own play dough. Let your imagination run wild without judgement. Playing with and in water in the warmer months.

Can any of you relate to my personal experience with a Narcissist in your life? Being so afraid, lonely, that you accepted to first person who payed you a compliment and took notice of you? I had been engaged to my previous partner for 2 years and considered myself a total failure because we didn't get married. Many years later I totally understand that if I had married him I wouldn't be the aware, and awake Starseed I am now!

Yes, I was desperate to have a man in my life, and that is what opens the door wide to the Narcissists. We are half apples, feeling so incomplete on our own, we are easy prey for them!

Remember, NOTHING IS EVER DONE TO US! WE CREATE IT ON A SOUL LEVEL FOR OUR OWN PERSONAL GROWTH LESSONS! Some of which are Karmic Soul Contracts from Past Lives where we will find the roles are reversed in this lifetime!

If any of you are beginning a new relationship and within the first few days they are telling you how deeply and madly they are falling in love with you, recognise it as a 95% chance it is total lies.

Get your running shoes on and get out of there as quick as possible!! They speak with silver tongues as they are really good con artists! My Narcissist looked so innocent, so deceptive. To look at him you would think butter would not melt in his mouth as the saying goes. Please, just beware!

Yes, I know, sometimes we have Soul Contracts with these people so in that instance we have to complete the contract with them and learn the lessons we have chosen to learn.

Since him I have had two long term relationships and am presently very happy on my own. I don't need anyone to make me feel whole and complete, I am whole and complete on my own which opens the door for my next partner to be whole and complete also. A much better relationship than two half apples I can reassure you. As long as you feel lonely on your own, you are still in half apple mode and have a lot of Inner Child work to do.

Well my life has just gone through a massive shift. I met a guy three years ago who was in a rebound relationship at the time, at Church. I discovered he was very much asleep so I added him to my FB friends so he could learn and grow, basically, wake up to what was going on. During those three years I ran from him energetically. He shared heaps of my posts and three years later FB recognised he was the person who had shared most of my posts. They unfriended us so a couple of days later we re friended each other. Next thing we knew our pages were invisible to each other. Neither of us are very IT skilled so it took me a while to find the blocked section, guess where I found him, so I unblocked him. In the meanwhile I got my friends whose posts I shared, to add him onto their pages so he could still share the posts. I wonder if they will realise we have been able to re friend each other again. I admit most of my friends on FB I do not know personally but him I do, very personally in fact. It makes me laugh, all I have to do is roll over to hug him. A friend of mine confirmed we are indeed Twin Flames. Of course he is Empathic, so much so that he can read my mind, so much for private thoughts! I have to keep reminding him I am not as skilled as he is in the field of Mental Telepathy so I still need him to speak to me. Mind you, I got quite a surprise today when I was having lunch, I suddenly realised there was a tear coming down my cheek from my right eye. I was fascinated and observed it in my thoughts for a while. I very rarely cry unless it is a sad movie or I am told someone I love dearly will be gently taken out of my life (my false Twin Flame whom I have known for ten years and we have experienced many Past Lives together). I thought we would always be a part of each other's lives but it is not to be.

I was so proud of my Twin Flame I sent him flowers on Valentine's Day, along with many of my other friends. At that stage I did not recognise him as my Twin Flame. It was funny, I could feel his energy getting closer and stronger but I still wanted to run even though he had been a very good student of mine. Later on he informed me that he had known three years ago that we were going to be together.

I didn't want to have a relationship with him when I found out his rebound relationship had ended as I was still friends with another man who had been in my life for ten years who was also asleep. I had enough on my plate dealing with one asleep man which is why I added him to my FB Page so he could learn, grow and most importantly WAKE UP! So funny, not long before my Twin Flame came back into my life all these videos about the runner in a Twin Flame relationship kept grabbing my attention. I was wondering why it was jumping out at me when, as far as I was concerned, I had not even met my Twin Flame. Yes, I was the Runner, big time! I would joke with my girlfriend in Couldville about having shares in Nike shoes because I was so good at running away from men once I identified a common theme with the men on the dating sites I was drawing to myself.

I have had many Past Lives with this man I had spent the last ten years with as friends. I thought I could help him to wake up. I had it confirmed in the last couple of years with him that he was also a Pleiadian Starseed. He is so very much asleep, in deep denial. Definitely in the "too hard basket" for him. Bless him he is also Psychic but would rarely allow these gifts to surface. Interestingly he had been on various Dating sites even before I met him, even when he was with his previous partner. He only recently told me that when he deleted my emails and discovered I was on Dating sites. Oh yes, Abandonment played a major part in our connection. I had been a boarder with him for three years but could no longer handle his drinking so when I came back from Couldville I got my own place.

Sadly many Pleiadian Starseeds turn to alcohol and drugs to cope being the "Black Sheep" of the family. Alcohol is his choice of escape. This was very challenging for me when I first connected to him as the Narcissist was also an alcoholic and I was deeply scarred from that experience as neither of my parents drank or smoked for that matter. I am a major passive smoker, so many people in my life have smoked.

Thankfully my Twin Flame does not smoke and only drinks small amounts rarely. He came up to a girlfriend's place to connect with me, nearly a three-hour drive for him. I was taking care of her cats, plants and house while she was away on a well-deserved cruise. Out of the blue my Twin Flame contacted me to let me know he had just found the flowers I had sent him on Valentine's Day through FB. He told me he had recently moved and that he was doing his washing. A couple of hours later I received a text asking for my address. He knew my home address although he hadn't been there for a long time. I was feeling cheeky so sent him my home address. My Guides stepped in and told me to give him the address of where I was staying, "fussy" I thought and laughed to myself, not really reading anything into it. A couple of hours later I get a phone call from him, "Where are you" I asked him. At the front door was his reply! Oh boy, did I panic, I was not expecting to see him!

In my world nothing happens until the time is right! He did mention to me that it was his belief we should have connected ages ago so I gently reminded him that the timing was not right back then.

That was on the 2nd March 2019. The 3rd March 2019 is a 333 numerologically. For me 333 is important, it is my connection to my Sky Family. Of course he is an AWAKE and AWARE Starseed, it was just the other stuff he wasn't aware of so I needed to share the awareness with him. I am quite amused by how many threes are involved in our connection! It was only last night that a girlfriend confirmed to me that he was indeed my Twin Flame! He is so Empathic he can read my mind!! No such thing as a private thought anymore! I was quite surprised today as mental telepathy is not a strong gift of mine, I was having lunch and suddenly became aware of a tear flowing down my cheek, followed by several others. Now this is extremely unusual as I rarely cry, usually just at sad movies or news. I just sat and noticed what was happening, recognising it was not my pain I was responding to, I rang my Twin Flame. He had been doing some research for a speech he was giving and discovered the guy he was doing the speech on had recently died. When I rang him, he admitted to just having "a moment". I was quite shocked that I had picked up on his emotions. All I have to do is tune in clearer to his words!

CHAPTER SEVEN

My Awakening Journey

Do you feel lost, bewildered, like you are a square peg trying desperately to fit into a round hole and cannot quite work out why it isn't working? Feeling so badly out of place but have no idea why? Do you ever wonder who dropped you off here and forgot to pick you up? You find yourself sitting outside looking at the stars and longing for "Home" but having no idea where it is. Even feeling slightly perturbed because it didn't make any logical sense to you why you were looking to the stars and feeling like "Home" was out there somewhere when, wasn't Earth your home?

Maybe you can relate to being the "Black Sheep" of the family. Maybe you are wondering if you were adopted and your parents forgot to tell you. Maybe there is a sense of total disconnect, like who are these people and where are my family? Are you extremely sensitive to Energy and your family just don't understand your sensitivity and think you are just putting on an act, after all, they aren't sensitive like you are and they just don't "get it!" Spending time on your own or with animals in Nature feels so wonderful. It is like you seem to be able to talk to the animals with your mind but nobody else in the family understands that and thinks you are a bit weird or crazy even. You try to explain how you feel to them but you might as well be talking to a brick wall, they have absolutely no understanding.

If this feels at all familiar to you, then I am here to tell you, you are not alone. I am aware it sure feels like it because us Starseeds were scattered far and wide, not all in the one place. I actually feel this was done for our safety on one level, so the dark energies couldn't bomb one area and kill us all off. The internet has been such a Blessing, allowing us all to connect from all over the world. I can bet that was not foreseen when it was created to collect our information

How many of you feel this nagging feeling that there is something really important that you are meant to be doing but you really don't understand what the details of this are. Does it feel sort of foggy, cloudy, not quite clear or like a jigsaw puzzle with massive areas that are not filled in as yet and you cannot seem to find the other pieces to put them together, they seem to be scattered over a wide area and sometimes you find a piece that fits into place but it is such a slow process. Do you feel frustrated, like you are bashing your head against a brick wall trying to find answers or people that understand you.

Once you find Meditation and learn to connect with your Higher Self, then answers seem to be more easily available. Then we often come across the stumbling block of Trust, and that is absolutely massive! We don't even trust our own Intuition and are so good at second guessing ourselves. When we do this things always fall apart of us and that really sucks and we find ourselves sliding into depression in many cases because things don't work out the way we wanted them to work out unfortunately!

Many of us are givers, "Rescuers" who run around after everyone else but remain totally invisible to ourselves and we don't even realise that we are invisible to ourselves. For many of us it is "normal" to put ourselves at the end of the line of priorities to attend to. When we don't listen to our Guides and slow down we are forced to slow down by them through becoming sick or some other situation which enforces us to rest and stop running around after others. Oh absolutely, guilt is a very familiar emotion to many of us. Playing "Blame post" is something many of us have done all of our lives, it is "normal" for us to do this! Sound familiar to anyone?

How many of you find your guts tied in knots because you feel worried or stressed? Just step back for a moment and look at what we worry and stress about, other adults behaviour or lack of it sound familiar to anyone or situations that fail to work out the way we wanted them to? How about situations, we are so good at wanting to control stuff that is not ours to control!

Interestingly a lot of us Rescuers are also Empathic. There are ten main types of Empaths.

Emotionally Receptive

Are very receptive of others emotional and physical states before they are expressed. This is one of the most common types of Empaths. You need to learn to differentiate between your emotions and those of others around you that you are picking up.

Physically Receptive / Medical Intuitive

You are receptive to the pains and illnesses of others. These Empaths often become Healers either in mainstream or alternative areas.

Claircognizant

These Empaths know if something needs to be done or if a person is telling the truth. You will pick up information about people purely being around them.

Geomantic / Environmental

These Empaths can sense if a natural disaster is impending.

Fanna

They can feel, hear and interact with animals.

Flora

Can communicate with plants through receiving their signals, you intuitively sense what a plant needs (green thumbs).

Precognitive

Can feel a situation or event before it happens, manifesting in the form of dreams of emotional or physical sensations.

Medium

Can either see, feel or hear Spirits.

Psychometric

Have the ability to receive energy, impressions and information from objects such as jewelry or photographs.

Telepathic

Can read another person's unexpressed thoughts.

Which Empath are you?? Can you relate to more than one of these Empathic abilities? It important you learn how to protect yourself energetically through the use of crystals or meditation so you don't end up in overwhelm. Spending time recharging in Nature can be very beneficial. Smokey Quartz and Tourmaline are very good protective stones for Empaths. It is a good idea to allow the crystals to choose you, tune into which ones are calling you. If you have an ABN number, in Australia, then you can go to Crystal Warehouses to get your Crystals. It was an amazing experience when my Twin Flame took me, we had a ball! The Shunghite Crystal which protects you from 5G Energies jumped at both of us so we got a necklace each to protect ourselves from destructive energies.

I have now got a very important question to ask you all, "Are we in charge of other adults behaviour?" No way!! That is their responsibility, not ours! They are not children after all, they need to grow up and face the consequences of their behaviour or lack of it! I admit, it is very hard when this affects us as well or children. How long are we going to change their nappies? Have you noticed as yet, they never change their behaviour when we do this anyway. It just gives them permission not to be a responsible person because they know you will do it for them! Honestly, how empowering is cleaning up their mess for them? Bottom line, it isn't! Hello, they are not 2 year old's! Even 2 year old's can be taught to pack their toys away! We dis-empower these adults when we do this for them, mind you, they will probably throw a 2 year old tantrum when we stop doing it. They have no interest in being responsible for themselves. Victims live in a "poor me mentality", they have no intention of taking personal responsibility for their behaviour! There are billions of us Rescuers willing to do that for them. This is their way of getting attention to themselves. Us Rescuers find it extremely difficult to be visible to ourselves so Victims play a very important part in our lives as they keep us distracted from our own hurt and pain.

Narcissists are major psychic vampires as well. They stay with us as long as we are supplying their needs, energetically, mentally, emotionally as well as physically.

Take a good look around you, how many adults are there for you as much as you are there for them? Are they energetically draining you? Is allowing this nurturing for yourself? I don't think so, it is like being run over by a steamroller, it leaves you feeling completely flat like a pancake!

Are any of you getting so frustrated by this behaviour from other adults you have put your foot down and learned a new magical word called NO? I know, it simply isn't a part of your vocabulary is it? Simply, "No, it is not convenient, end of story!" Now when we have an abusive Narcissist in our lives, which us Empaths are very good at doing, using No can be very tricky as they have a habit of getting extremely abusive both verbally and physically. I know about this, I had one in my life for 17 years before I finally got free from him. One thing they are very good at doing is bringing us to "Crash and Burn" where we eventually become visible to ourselves but oh man, us Rescuers can do stubborn real well. We need the immense pain the Narcissist gives us before we finally become visible to ourselves.

I know the fear they give you, threats of killing you, which sadly many Empaths are killed by their Narcissistic partners, I was very nearly one so I know about these things.

It is not till the fear of staying in the violent situation becomes greater than the fear of leaving, that you find the courage to escape. I strongly suggest you get the police involved and get a Restraining Order / Intervention Order. Now there will be some Narcissists, like the one that was in my life, that have absolutely no respect for the law at all. Knowing this, I had to leave my home that I was buying, he never saw that coming, he thought he had me trapped but guess what, he was wrong, very wrong indeed! In cases like mine, you need to go into Refuge for your own safety!

Maybe you are aware of how the Narcissist puts one mask on for people who are on the outside of the dotted line they put around themselves. People on the outside of the dotted line think the Narcissist is the total opposite from what they are like behind closed doors with their family. People on the outside of the dotted line will accuse you of being a liar if you try to explain to them what the true nature of the monster you live with is. Be prepared, the Narcissist is very good at turning your family and friends away from you. When you do leave, you cannot tell ANYONE where you are once you leave that house!

Sadly I was witness to one lady who contacted her Narcissist partner while she was in Refuge because she was scared of being on her own. He promised her he would never abuse her again, he kept his promise for 3 days then treated her twice as bad as he did before because she dared to leave! Luckily she was able to escape again, she learned the lesson well that you cannot trust anything that comes out of their mouths! To put it mildly, they speak with forked tongue as the Native Americans would say! In other words they dribble heaps of BS. They are often gifted with the "Gift of the Gab" which is what sucks people in and keeps them blind to the true character of these very dangerous people!

Sadly there are many people who are terrified of being on their own, these people will put up with shocking abuse within a relationship rather than be on their own until the scales tip and the fear of being in the abusive relationship is greater than the fear of being on their own. The threat of being murdered is a good trigger to tip the scales, it sure worked for me!

Some Empaths find themselves hospitalised with the physical abuse they receive and they still go back to their partners. Yes, I did that as well so I totally understand why people do this! FEAR is a powerful motivator indeed!

We just need to keep in mind, nothing happens until the time is right!

CHAPTER EIGHT

My main relationships

Firstly when I was 16 years old I met the father of my daughter. We were introduced by a guy who had been on a trip we had been on in Tasmania, he had videoed a lot of places and activities we had experienced that holiday.

On the Queen's Birthday weekend he was taking David across to family in Adelaide when he stayed with us for a few days. David was also very shy. We found it easy to talk to each other and I felt very comfortable with him. He lived 2 hours away from me so we would write letters to each other. He gave me his signet ring to wear, that made me feel very special. I grew up a Catholic so I knew nothing about Psychic ability but I KNEW with every cell in my body I was going to have a daughter with him.

The next extremely significant relationship I had was with a Scottish boy who lived down the end of my street. I was 17 at the time. His sister was a good friend of mine. Billy passed over when he was 20 in a motor bike accident, 44 years later he still walks with me. He told me I have taught him about love, it didn't matter to me that he was no longer here physically, I still feel his energy very strongly. He has his ways of making himself known to me, keeping in mind, I am Psychic! Once again, Abandonment played a major part in my relationship with him. He did move to Ararat before I went to Tramville so I lost contact with him on the physical. Through friends Billy found out where I was living in Tramville so he came to see me. I was engaged to Rudy by the time he found me. He spent the night with us and in the morning stole our rent money! I was so embarrassed, ashamed and so furious at him! Interestingly fifteen years later he came through at church. It took me a while before I was able to get an answer from him as to why he had stolen the money. His reason was Rudy had stolen something that belonged to him so he then stole something that belonged to Rudy in revenge for Rudy being with me. I guess I was never meant to be on the back of his bike, I have far too much work to do here. Billy did some extra training on the other side to become one of my middle grandsons Guides. Billy had a deal with Cooper, that whenever I was around, Cooper would step aside and allow Billy to come through his body so he could spend time with me. As a result, Cooper does not know me.

I am deeply grateful to Cooper for allowing Billy to come through and spend time with me. David and I lost contact for many years, reconnecting through friends in similar circles. I was engaged to Rudy then so several more years passed and I had divorced the Narcissist I had married. Being with a Narcissist, another example of Abandonment equals Love!

David and I were reconnected once again., sixteen years later. This time we were both single. I must admit I was shocked the first time we made love I didn't fall pregnant. I remember thinking, there is something wrong here, I clearly remembered I was going to have his daughter. Second time lucky. I had a perfect pregnancy with her. She gave me the love that her father didn't know how to. I thought I could love him enough it didn't matter he couldn't love me, I was happy when he came and spent time with us. Another example of Abandonment equals Love!

Thirty two years after she was born, he came through at Church in Evidence of Survival, I had spoken to him about being a Spiritualist. The medium would bring through unusual names, she called out his surname, I claimed him immediately. My daughter never really got to know her father and as an adult was very angry at him for not being there for her. I had tried tracking him down a year or so before he passed over and let his ex-neighbour, whom he seemed to spend a lot of time with, know that he had 5 grandchildren.

Rudy is a Dutch man, we were engaged for 2 years. I had my 21st birthday with him. My Mum wore a navy blur kaftan with tulips on it, there was a pot of tulips on the table as well and they even brought my girlfriend Sandy with them so she could celebrate with me. Mum's sister in law made me an amazing 21st cake which was photographed for prosperity. Her husband, Uncle Lyn, mum's brother was such a beautiful man and he was there also as well as my precious sister. Rudy was a very social person, I was very shy, I was so jealous and possessive of him that damaged our relationship severely. I guess the straw that broke the camel's back was when I fell pregnant to him. He had a low sperm count so didn't believe he could have children. I suffered severely with morning sickness so the doctor put me on Debendox tablets. I found out many years later that Debendox was more damaging than Thalidimide so Peter would have been born severely damaged but he had chosen to grow up on the other side of life. He is one of my daughter's Guides. I was so depressed after my abortion, upset hormones, I tried to commit suicide. That was it for Rudy, he spoke to the doctor then walked out of my life. Peter came through at Church and gave me his name. Billy took care of him when I was awake, I cared for him when I was asleep. I was guided to go to an Evidence of Survival meeting many years later with a medium Jackie whom I worked with. Both Billy and Peter came through to bring me messages. Pete was sitting on Billy's knee, it was so beautiful.

Micheal is Irish, an alcoholic and a Narcissist. I felt like a massive failure because I had failed to get married and I was so desperately lonely so when Michael began paying me attention and putting me up on a pedestal I fell for it hook line and sinker! It is through our deep loneliness that they are able to glide into our lives. Their Love Equation is Abandonment, Control and Abuse which needs to align with our own Love Equation.

Some of you Empaths may have also had the challenging experience of bringing a Narcissist into your lives making your lives hell on Earth, it is a karmic experience. We only become visible to ourselves when we "crash and burn", otherwise we lick our wounds for a few days then go back to being used by the Victims around us. It took me 17 years to finally be free from this man!

Narcissists place us on a pedestal and when we feel happy and comfortable they proceed to destroy us emotionally, nothing we do is good enough, and we are often physically abused as well. They threaten to kill us, as in my case, if we leave. When we do escape, they turn our friends and family against us. You see, they have a dotted line around them, people on the outside of that dotted line think butter wouldn't melt in their mouths but once you are on the inside of that dotted line, it is like Jeckel and Hyde, man you see a very ugly side of them but nobody believes you! You spend your life "walking on eggshells", never knowing what is going to upset them next

I guess it was my feeling of being a failure, feeling incomplete because I had failed to get married to Rudy that made me so vulnerable to needing someone in my life to make me feel whole and complete. Oh man, please take note, when you hear bells with these partners, believe me, they are WARNING bells!!! Please take heed of them! Okay, as a Spiritualist I understand Karmic contracts and Past Life and that on a Soul Level, we ask these people to play these roles so we can learn lessons. We are so extremely vulnerable when we feel like this and fall for their advances like a camel who has been without water and has just found an Oasis! Literally, some Empaths are killed by the Narcissists in their lives through total and utter rage. Thankfully for me I learned to listen to my Guides who were telling me I needed to leave my home immediately and Michael was on the phone saying he wasn't coming home but I knew he was lying! The Narcissist is extremely good at lying. I got a call from a friend telling me her Guides were telling her to contact me as well to offer a safe place for us to go as we were unsafe where we were so I was very well looked after or I wouldn't be here writing this book.

Seventeen years of physical and mental abuse, walking on eggshells through fear of not knowing what the next thing he was going to do. I received couple of minced mouths from him, of course he told his mother and uncle that I was having problems with my wisdom teeth! He would call me all the time so I had to make sure I was home to answer the phone or all hell would break loose when he got home! They are major control freaks! Another thing he was very good at was taking "sickies" He would have me ring his boss with the excuse he had given me then would drill me for hours over what the bosses response on the phone was. When he was drunk he would continually play the record of Key Largo. I hadn't heard it for years but was instantly transported back in time to the flat we lived in when he did this. Champaign Cocktails allowed the monster in him to really come out full blast! I was a nervous wreck around alcohol as my parents never drank so I didn't know what to expect or how to act without upsetting him. After that first time, every time we went out and he ordered them I would literally begin shaking and then my son would feel the tension and start screaming which made him worse. Unfortunately babies are not dolls and they do not come with batteries. I forgot to mention, my sister is 16 months younger than me so I knew nothing about physically comforting a crying baby. Me being so stressed certainly didn't help my son at all. The monster would keep screaming at me to shut the baby up, I felt like I was in hell. At that stage I was still a Catholic and I firmly believed hell had come to me while I was still alive, the monster was also a Catholic.

My next partner Theo was also an Empath and his wife was the Narcissist. I had tarred all men with the same brush by the time I escaped from Michael so I guess I needed to understand that women were also Narcissists. I guess this was a Healing relationship for both of us. Theo was the male role model for my daughter from when she was 9 years old. Her brother had left home before Theo had come into our lives. My daughter was very protective of me and they had a massive battle between them deciding who was going to be my main protector. I was basically a basket case since my son walked out of my life when he was 16, three weeks after we were relocated through Refuge. Theo was also a Psychic so I told him to get his own place and I was moving interstate to be with the man I was meant to be with. I was so severely put off by the Porn movies he use to watch, made me sick! He developed some weird behaviours I really didn't feel comfortable with which is why I separated from him. He was half German, half Dutch. I was very grateful to Theo for reconnecting me with the Good Red Road. I have several Native American Past Lives.

Several years after I relocated I connected with a German man who was 11 years my junior. Gunter is a workaholic and a heavy drinker. I was terrified of anyone who drank but my daughter kept telling me not everyone who drinks is violent and abusive. It took me many years before I was able to take that thought on board as I had been so damaged by my first experience with a drinker. Neither of my parents drank and neither did I except maybe on my birthday, a couple of glasses of wine and that was it! We have just celebrated 10 years of friendship. I boarded with him for three years but couldn't handle his everyday drinking and his blackouts. I love living on my own and am definitely a whole apple, not needing someone in my life but leaving the door open if another whole apple would like to join me. I am thrilled I have recently been able to connect with his teenage Lover whom he asked to marry when he was going to live up at Emerald but she turned him down. That part of him is still very much in love with her. Spirit told me there was a younger woman coming into his life, he didn't believe me saying no Reading he has ever had has come true so I would need to bring her in, so I did with Spirit's help of course. Gunter still wants to marry her, they both feel lonely so are still half apples, I believe they have a Soul Contract together to heal and grow. I was surprised a couple of nights ago when she contacted me to wish me all the best on my 10 year anniversary with Gunter.

Three hours later, she is saying she feels we could be great friends and that she would love to help me any way she can. She is a full on Rescuer as well. She arranged to come and physically meet me and go out for lunch. Apparently she rang Gunter and told him we had been talking so he rang me at 1am to ask what had we been discussing so I read out the messages we had written to each other. I told Gunter at the beginning when he mentioned to me that he wanted to marry her, that I would happily walk Sandy down the aisle, she is estranged from her father and her mother passed over when she was 17.

I would call her mother in energetically and invite her to walk with us. I see this as being the most beautiful Wedding Gift I could give to them. That part of him that asked her to marry him is well and truly on the surface, I am very pleased to see him so happy as my contract with him is over and it is time once again for me to move on.

Every time Sandy got drunk she would break up with Gunter. Finally after six months the relationship was over for good. When I brought Sandy into his life I did tell him I was going to have a man coming into my life as well. He didn't believe me, thinking I was far too different from most people and that I would never find someone who resonated with me.

Well much to his shock and disappointment I have now connected to my Twin Flame. They both know about each other and as my Twin Flame has the gift of Mental Telepathy he has read Gunter's mind as well as mine and knows that I love Gunter deeply due to the many Past Lives we have had together but there is no way I can do a relationship with him in this life.

My Twin Flame and I have a lot of work to do together. Yes, he has put a Labradorite ring on my finger much to the delight of our Pleiadian Family.

He has been aware of the Ships since he was a child and has been able to communicate with them. That is something way beyond Gunter's ability to grasp or acknowledge. Bless him he lives in denial because the TRUTH is too much for him to digest presently.

CHAPTER NINE

My Reflections

The way us Rescuers / Empaths open ourselves up to bringing these people into our lives on a physical level is through LONLINESS. Feeling incomplete on our own! Of course we also need to remember that on a Soul level we set up these Soul Contracts because we are so good at being invisible to ourselves! The only way we become visible is when we crash and burn! We need to hurt and hurt really badly to finally become visible to ourselves.

I grew up with very strict boundaries so my Inner Child was very use to strict boundaries. Being put up on a Pedestal felt so good, he hooked me in so firmly. Once you feel secure on that pedestal, they then begin tearing it down, leaving you wondering what on earth you have done wrong and continually trying to get back up there. What we need to remember is a Narcissist has absolutely no Empathy and they are all about Service to Self! Making people miserable brings them so much satisfaction. This is something us Empaths have extreme difficulty in understanding.

I had come back from 6 months overseas travelling through England, Scandinavia, Russia, Europe, Spain, Portugal and Morocco. I had even stayed in Holland on my own for 10 days, eight of which were in a small hamlet where Rudy was born. I went back to working at the After Care Hospital where Michael had become a Porter in my absence. The Matron even tried to stop me from being in a relationship with him so I resigned!

He was three years younger than me and had such a "baby" face, so innocent looking, like butter wouldn't melt in his mouth. He dressed really well. It wasn't long before the split personality came to the surface, in front of strangers he was pleasant and caring, behind closed doors he was totally the opposite! His father died when he was 15 and his mother was an alcoholic so he took over the control of the family. He would bash her up every time she got stuck in the pub and forgot to pick his siblings up from school. I soon learned that his family did what he told them. I was 22 when I met him, I had my 22nd birthday in the middle of the Sahara Desert, finally getting into Meninski Oasis at 10 p.m. that night. The bus had broken down. He convinced his family to tell me he was turning 21. I thought it was strange there was no big celebration happening but they were poor. His mother would have been on a Widows Pension supplemented by his income. We finally got a place of our own and we got a puppy. Well he squeezed that dog so badly its bowel fell out through the anus, I was horrified I was beginning to see how cruel he was. He told me he had arranged for it to go to a farm so it had plenty of room to run around. I believed him but now, knowing what I know about how violent he was, I would not be surprised if he didn't dump it somewhere or even kill it. Makes my skin crawl just thinking about it. The pup would sleep under the sheets by my feet. We only had him a couple of weeks. I adored him which probably made the Narcissist jealous which was probably why he hurt it so badly.

We had planned to get married on Valentine's Day the next year but we had a massive argument. To make up to me he promised we would get married as soon as it could be arranged. All these bells went off in my head, I thought they were wedding bells, WRONG!! They were warning bells big time!

We had planned to get married in the Botanical Gardens but didn't realise we had to get permission to do that so we ended up getting married in front of the War Memorial. Oh man, that set the energy for the remainder of our life together! Chaos, fighting, tantrums, from him, the atmosphere was so thick you needed a chain saw to cut through it! Of course it was a Soul Contract, I wasn't aware of symbolism at that stage. I remember at the motel where we had the reception, in our room, Mum would empty the glasses of alcohol as soon as someone put it down. Probably had a lot to do with why he went out with his mate so he could well and truly get drunk.

On our wedding night he went out with one of the other porters from the hospital. I remember feeling massively abandoned in the motel room alone. I don't even remember him coming back, I remember feeling so confused. The next day there was pressure to get the wedding photos before my dress had to be returned. I had paid for the veil.

We got another place close to his Mum. I remember we were using a condom and it burst, The next morning I went over to his Mum and told her I was pregnant, she asked me how far, I said, last night!

I was so uneducated as far as pregnancy was concerned, so after that we didn't use a condom and yes, there was a positive pregnancy test after my moon cycle failed to arrive.

He refused to allow me to go to prenatal classes so when I went into labour I had no idea what to expect. I remember them shaking me and telling me I could push. I had no urge to do so at all. My Mum bless her had come over to Adelaide to be with me as I was giving birth.

I was late so they were to induce me. I was in a 4-bed ward and was the last one induced, I was an emotional mess. I was well and truly ready to give birth to my son.

He was a colicky baby so would scream for ages before going to sleep. Michael would constantly scream at me to shut him up, like he came with an instruction manual on how to turn down the volume.

He didn't even come with batteries that I could take out! I had never taken care of a baby before this although I did a Mothercraft course at High School. I still remember how overwhelmed I felt. Nurses suggested giving them a bath to settle them down, not my son, he hated being bathed! Wasn't too thrilled about having his nappy being changed, this would be another reason for him to start screaming, maybe he didn't like the cold air. This went on for ages.

Michael thought it would be easy taking care of a baby so sent me out to work. I get this phone call telling me to come straight home, he cannot stop our son from screaming. We lived on the first floor of flats, I get home to my baby being in his pram sitting on the apron of the flats screaming himself senseless. Apparently Michael had placed him in his bouncer and had tripped over it! Anthony refused to go anywhere near his bouncer after that.

We went back to Tramville when he was three months old and moved in with his mother who was also taking care of her daughter's baby born a month beforehand. Anthony was born in March, by Father's Day we were in Refuge for the first time, the first one in Tramville.

Michael had a habit of calling Locum doctors to give him Morphine when he was really drunk. The place we were living he would lock us in the flat while he went to work. We had no landline in the flat so in order for him to ring the locum we had to go down to the end of the street. He could hardly walk so I took advantage of it and just ran till I got into the city and the main police station, talk about being pumped up on Adrenaline. We spent the night in the Watch house before being taken to the Refuge. While we were there a lady came in with two children who had conjunctivitis, it quickly spread to the rest of the kids and some of the adults. Stressed people get sick very easily. After several months I was placed into a Ministry of Housing flat in a massive complex of high rise flats.

Michael had the gift of the gab, a total expert in lying! I am amazed he remembered who he told what lie to. If he was caught out he was always good at thinking on his feet and quickly create another lie to cover up the first one! He convinced Social Security to give him the details of where I was. Can you imagine the shock and terror I felt when I saw him standing at the door. He forced me to pack my stuff up and go back home with him promising that things would change. Well they did get better for like three days then things got twice as bad!

Just a note of extreme warning to all those Empath / Rescuers in Refuge, if your loneliness gets the better of you and you contact your abuser, just be aware they are really mad at you for leaving so will sweet talk you into coming back. For a couple of days things may improve but it won't be long before things are twice as bad as they were before you left! They do not like it when you escape their control!!

It is my personal belief that all these domestic murders you hear of are out of control Narcissists being furious at us Empath / Rescuers. Remember that before you try to contact your Narcissistic partners! You left an extremely abusive situation for a very good reason, your life may literally have depended on it!!I cannot emphasise this strongly enough!

When we went out and he started drinking if anyone looked at him sideways he would get into a punch on with them. He was always fighting his younger brother who eventually moved to Perth to get away from him. He would force myself and our young son to get in the car with him when he couldn't even walk a straight line, that was terrifying. He would often go into rages when he was driving, bashing the steering wheel and going all over the road. It was such a nightmare, I know I was looked after very well during this time by my Guides and Loved ones on the other side!

One day when I was pregnant a car hit us from behind as we were turning across another two lanes of traffic, forcing us to hit another car. I ended up in hospital being unable to walk for a while. It was during this hospital stay that my mother realised I was being abused physically as well as emotionally. The Insurance people cut the car in half and expected me to pay for it instead of putting it in as a write off, very shonky I believed! It was totally unsafe, there was no way I wanted that car back! So I set up a payback plan that suited me. I never picked the car up!

The second time I managed to escape I was working in Aged Care and my son was still in nappies, They allowed me to live in the Nurses Home but wouldn't allow me to keep my son with me so they arranged for someone to care for him in their home 24/7. I only got to see him on my days off. It was a long bus drive. I don't even remember now how I ended up back with Michael again. I do remember when we picked Anthony up he had a sore underneath his penis. I felt so bad that he wasn't being well taken care of. Yes, obviously there are quite a few blackout periods.

His mum use to say, "The closer the alter, the greater the rogue!" I had no idea at the time what she was talking about but she obviously knew about the paedophilia which didn't start becoming public knowledge for many years after she died.

The idea of confession where a husband would be beating his wife for example, would go to Confession, confess his sins, say a few prayers then go home and bash his wife again, really didn't make any sense to me. That is one of the reasons why I left the Catholic church plus the 30-year war in Ireland between the Orange and the Green, Protestants and Catholics, really made no sense to me! After all, were they not both Christian religions? Wasn't the Christian bible the same for all Christian religions and why were there so many different Christian religions, that didn't make any sense to me either.

It made me wonder what the common denominator was underneath all the Christian religions to start with and then, what if there was a common denominator under ALL religions and that thought led me on my journey to become a Spiritualist. Spiritualism accepts all pathways as ways to learn lessons. None of this, I am right and you are wrong division, rather, you are learning the lessons you have chosen to learn by following your own pathway and this goes for the atheists as well. For absolutely EVERYONE! The Lakota Sioux have a saying, Mitakuye Oyasin, which loosely means WE ARE ONE! That is definitely my perception!

Enough of the divisions that have been created between us, do we all not bleed when we cut ourselves? Do we not all have the same organs in our bodies? The colour of our skin, our different languages all create divisions between us. Can we not see past these surface expressions and realise we all need oxygen to breathe! It does not matter what our skin colour is or how much money we have, deprive us of oxygen and none of us will live for very long.

Talking about oxygen, you do realise trees breathe in carbon dioxide and give out oxygen which brings me to ponder, why is mankind so focused on destroying trees that we need for oxygen? Just a side thought to ponder, have we had enough of breathing? Never mind what destroying the habitat of wild animals does for them, but then there are people in power who only think about money.

What a shame they cannot breathe it for example, or even eat it if it comes to that point. Don't get me started on Monsanto and Bayer genetically modifying and poisoning our foods! Off my soap box for now, lol

CHAPTER TEN

My Healing Journey

Surrender, Trust, Patience and learning when to let go are such massive lessons for us to learn.

How many times do we second guess ourselves, get confused and then go by what we analysed to have everything just fall apart on us ? Then we find ourselves scratching our heads trying to work out why everything doesn't go the way we thought it was going to! It is my understanding that we cannot walk through new doorways until we shut the old one for example looking for a new relationship while we are still in the old one! Feeling incomplete unless we have a relationship is a sure fire way of bringing the Abandonment issue into the new relationship. Being "half an apple" will only bring in another half apple. There is a Universal Law that states like attracts like so I have a suggestion. How about you connect with a Professional to guide you through your Inner Child work so you can become whole and complete on your own, that way you will attract a partner who has also worked on themselves.

Two 'whole apples' make a much better relationship than two half ones. When you do this your new partner will be there for you as much as you are there for them! In order for you to become whole and complete may I suggest you become like the caterpillar and go within your cacoon while you go through your massive changes. Learn to put some boundaries up, learn a new magical word called

NO and use it on the people who are never there for you when you need assistance. Just a suggestion, up to you whether you do it or not.

The prerequisite for being strong enough to do this is massive amounts of PAIN! Otherwise we tend to be totally invisible to ourselves, only able to give, and find it extremely hard to receive! In many many cases we can trace this back to our childhoods where we took on board the belief system which says, "I don't deserve!" Sound familiar to anyone? Becoming a parent to ourselves is what doing our Inner Child work is all about.

This brings me to a very challenging lesson of Forgiveness. I know this will probably do your heads in hardcore, mind you I am not saying forget but learn the lesson that on a Soul level you asked this person to play so we can grow Spiritually! It is very important to understand that when we do not want to forgive someone, that doesn't cause them any pain at all! On the other hand it causes us immense amounts of damage, mentally, emotionally and in some cases where it is deep enough we can even cause ourselves physical problems due to the stress we carry because of this. The reason why we Forgive is for OUR HEALTH! It has nothing to do with the other person!

On a Soul Level I believe we ask these people to play these roles so we can learn certain lessons such as Trust and Forgiveness! In my world, we are Spirit having a human experience, this is a school of life!

I would like to present you with something different. Take yourselves out of Victim mode, 'poor me' and recognise that nothing in this life is EVER done to us! These people are purely actors and actresses playing a role, that we ourselves asked them to play on a Soul level, so we can Spiritually Grow. Like going up to the next class in school. Is this making any sense to you?

You see I believe that when we don't forgive, it isn't making any difference to the person we are not forgiving, but may I suggest, it is doing ourselves a massive amount of damage with all the hate, anger, resentment etc that we hold onto. I believe this eats away at us emotionally and mentally and I believe we can make ourselves extremely sick! This is the reason why we forgive! It has nothing to do with the other person who just played out a role we asked them to, it is for our HEALTH, literally!

How many of you stress and worry so much you end up with headaches or even migraines? I don't know about you but pain and me really don't get on together very well at all, I have a very low pain threshold!

Have you heard of the saying, 'Let Go and let God'? I find it very useful, understanding it is my thoughts and my beliefs which have a big influence in our lives, of course along with the lessons we set up for ourselves along the way.

I just find it handy stepping back and looking at my life like I am looking at a movie and asking my Higher Self, my Guides, God, whoever you see as the Highest Spiritual Source, "Please help me to remember the lesson I chose to learn through creating this situation, thank you!" If we were perfect we would learn our lessons the first time around but we are not perfect or we wouldn't be here in this school of life. Be gentle with yourselves, stop giving yourselves a hard time! Put down those clubs you keep bashing yourselves over the head with because you made a "mistake". No you didn't, it was just a lesson!

I believe the biggest lesson I have needed to learn is to give myself permission to be a Student of Life! We have held out dated patterns and beliefs since childhood. When we are trying to change them, of course we will occasionally slip back into old behaviour patterns. When we realise we have done this, congratulate yourself instead of bashing yourself over the head because you cannot change anything if you are unaware of it!

I have found a brilliant way to discover what belief patterns are affecting our lives is to sit quietly and observe our thought patterns. They are all snugly tucked away in our sub conscious mind. Since we cannot change anything we are not aware of this is a wonderful way of bringing those buried beliefs to the surface. Once we have identified them, remember release any judgement! Take a note of them then turn them around to positive statements in the present tense! Using I am now or I now have, brings whatever you put in after it into the present tense. Now remember these thought patterns / beliefs have been with us for many years, sometimes decades, so the reality we are experiencing will take several months of constant hand writing, one page every day. Patience is one of the lessons we choose to learn and it certainly comes into play when we are doing this. The change we desire takes just a tad longer than a weekend to manifest and will do so gradually when it happens. No point writing it for a weekend then throwing your hands up in the air declaring it doesn't work! We need to do it for several months at a minimum! Hand writing connects to the sub conscious!

A lot of us Empaths are also Rescuers and as Rescuers we try to "fix" people which never works by the way! The bottom line is the only person we can "fix" is OURSELVES! Well we tend to be major control freaks because of our need to be needed. When we find ourselves confused we have been second guessing ourselves instead of trusting what we are receiving from our Guides, our Intuition if you like.

As Rescuers we are extremely invisible to ourselves due to our long held belief we got from childhood that we don't deserve. This is why we are extremely good at Giving and very bad at Receiving. Learning to do "nice" for us is a massive challenge which is why this trip to Couldville was so important to me as it had been a burning desire of mine for so long. I felt extremely depressed at the thought of never getting to do it because my partner wanted me to buy a house, which to me really was not important.

Keeping in mind that whatever we are given in the first 7 years of our lives is what we take on board as "Love". If there is abuse, chaos, Abandonment, that is what we bring into our adult relationships! We think we want tender loving care and support but we don't get it!

Sadly many of us have grown up with a parent who is a Narcissist. In this case, the emotional and physical abuse is so "normal" that when we experience that abuse with our partners it can take many years before we get to a point of even thinking that something is wrong in our relationship!

In this case the Empath / Rescuer is sometimes even murdered by their partner because they are so use to extreme abuse they don't hear the warning bells going off in their heads.

We never leave our relationships until the pain of being on our own is less than the pain of being in an abusive relationship. The more abusive our childhood, whether it was happening to us as children or even if we just observed one parent abusing the other one The programming we get from Society is that our parents "Love" us. Sadly this "Love" is often not tender loving care and support. It is often Abandonment (created in single parent families, also created when one or both parents are workaholics, or cannot emotionally communicate).

Where a Narcissist is a parent then our "Love Equation' often includes substance abuse, anger, sulking, physical and emotional abuse. The children often learn how to lie and that lying is normal in that environment. As a result if they don't lie themselves then they may bring someone in who does lie (probably a Narcissist)

Our Inner Child then goes looking for a partner to love us, in the same way we were loved as a child. When we become teenagers we often read Romance Novels and we think that is the love we are looking for but if we never experienced that as a child, our Inner child doesn't recognise that as "Love!" This can mess with our heads so severely when the dream love and the actual love are poles apart!

We are often invisible to ourselves, we take on board the belief that we don't deserve due to many factors, parents being poor, abuse both verbal and physically are massive influences creating these realities. Even in wealthy families where children are sent to Boarding schools and are brought up by Nannies, they also have Abandonment as their love equation because their parents are too busy working all the time.

My parents grew up during the Depression, for them it was important to own their own home so they both worked, my sister and I were "latch key kids". Mum was big on lists so we had a list of what we were to be doing for every day of the week from when we woke up to when we went to bed! We grew our own vegetables, had our own chooks and had a couple of cows. Bringing the cows up and milking them every morning was one of our duties. The Common where we had the cows was just down the end of our street. We had a Jersey, she was very gentle, her name was Madge, and an Ayrshire, her name was Beauty and she was very nervy, highly strung. She was on heat one day and refused to come up to be milked, plus the bull was hanging around and I was terrified of the Bull. Anyway, she picked me up with her horns and carried me for quite a distance. I was still in Primary school yet this is still as clear with me as though it was just yesterday. We had to be very careful going in through the fence as it was barbed wire! You really knew about it if you got the point of one of those barbs, and there was so many to choose from!.

Many years later I got to milk a cow when my daughter went to Kindergarten, I never forgot how to do it. We hand milked, no milking machines for us and our hands would cramp up several times before we had finished milking the first cow. We would bring them into the shed and they would be feeding of course while we milked them. We needed to be careful Beauty didn't kick the bucket over. The walk home with a full bucket of milk made the walk ten times further, that metal bucket was heavy enough empty! At school, we use to have bottled milk delivered. Being a milk monitor was fun but they use to leave the milk out on the sun too long at times before the milk crates were brought inside. We would use a metal like knitting needle to put a hole in the foil tops and then put the straws in.

Due to the fact we had our own cows Mum gave us an excuse note so we didn't have to drink the Pasteurised milk because we were only use to fresh milk. We would make our own butter as well with a hand beater! Oh man, my arms want to drop off at the mere thought of it still!!It seemed to take forever for the cream to turn into butter. We had wooden butter pats with the lines in the paddles.

We would drink the butter milk We thought dripping on toast with a bit of salt was a special treat. We grew Nasterchums in the front yard and would have the leaf in sandwiches, man they were peppery so you just had a single leaf and lots of butter!. Tick-Toc biscuits were a special treat and encouraged us how to tell the time as well, no digital clocks in those days. They had different coloured icing on top and on the back was a clock face with various different times. If you could tell what the time was, you got to eat the biscuit!

I remember one day my sister and I were under a table, someone was taking care of us, and we ate the whole packet of Tic-Tocs. I think we had the measles at the time. The adults were extremely unimpressed, we got into a lot of trouble for doing that. Another day under the table again, I got hold of some scissors and cut my sisters long hair, that went down like a lead balloon, I gave her a fringe.

As a Spiritualist it is my belief that we are more than this flesh and blood. We are children of God and God is Spirit, therefore we are also Spirit. I see the Earth Plane as a School of Life where we come to learn lessons such as Patience, Forgiveness, Surrender and Trust. How many of you have learnt Patience for example. I know that is a lesson I am still working on so in my understanding how can we possibly learn all these lessons in one lifetime? My understanding is that we keep Reincarnating until we have not only learnt these lessons but cleared the Karma we create with certain other Souls so people we have had relationship with in Past Lives we often reconnect with again in the next life to work out our Karma.

It took me 17 years to finally get the Narcissist out of my life and to be free from the abuse. For me the experience was like living in extreme anxiety, walking on "eggshells", never knowing what was going to upset him next. They get so much pleasure in seeing you suffer! I actually went into Woman's Refuge on two different occasions because he was a private detective and kept finding me. Just a word to the wise, when you leave, NEVER TELL ANYONE because your family and friends are the first people the Narcissist will go to when they are looking for you and by telling them you are putting both them and yourself in danger!

The Narcissist in my life was so "tuned into me" he walked up to me three hours after I had gone to have lunch with friends in a busy shopping centre! That was how strong the soul connection was between us! In the end I escaped by changing my vibration.

This process to escape the Narcissist in your life takes a massive amount of courage because they often threaten to kill you or other family members if you leave. That really messes with your head massively and makes you a virtual prisoner to them.

Tools I found useful after I left the Narcissist

I strongly suggest getting some Counselling to assist you in recovering from the Narcissistic abuse many of you will have suffered since childhood. Not just any Counsellor, they need to be a Specialist in the field of Narcissistic Abuse and Inner Child work. Something you need to realise when you have to go NO CONTACT with everyone, you WILL go through deep, and extremely intense grieving and feel so alone and lost. This is another reason you must get Counselling as soon as possible!

Remember, someone does not have to die for you to grieve, you can grieve for any type of loss, work, house, pets, friendships etc. The longer you have had the association with a particular person, place or thing, the longer and deeper the grieving process! It isn't something you complete in a weekend

Just like your Emotional Healing work, it may take years! Look at the Healing / grieving process as working your way down through the layers of an onion. There are many layers before you reach the core issue and that can take a lot of intense work to dissolve that itself! A few sticks of dynamite figuratively speaking, to break apart that initial incident which caused the hurt and pain in the first place.

The sub conscious mind is very good at blacking out situations in order for you to cope with life for example sexual abuse is often blacked out for decades. The "skeletons" in the family closest such as sexual abuse, are often generational sadly. What we need to remember is that whatever we are given in the first 7 years of our life is what we take on board as "Love". Incest is one of the patterns that are passed down from one generation to the next but it is never spoken off because it is "their little secret" the child is told, hence it gets blacked out often. I have been aware of partners of mine that have also been sexually abused, in some cases I have been aware they have sexually abused their siblings. Sometimes it goes right through the extended family to cousins, Aunts, Uncles and Grandparents.

I was watching a video recently of this 40 year old man who had been doing a lot of emotional healing work on himself and was just beginning to have memories as a four year old of having a man taking his hand and telling him that "this was their little secret!" This sort of thing happens far more frequently than we would like to admit. Thankfully a lot is now being exposed, especially in the Catholic church! They have a ritual called "Confession" where they go and admit their sins to a priest who gives them some prayers to say and they are magically absolved of their sins. They then go home and continue the abuse they just went to Confession to admit to. It is a never ending cycle of knowing they can commit a "sin", and just go to Confession and be absolved!

It is a scam in my opinion, no personal responsibility in that pattern whatsoever!

David Icke has some very interesting views on what happens in the Illuminati which the Catholic church is heavily involved in according to him. Well it is now public knowledge that a lot of members of the Catholic Church are Pedos. I have seen articles where the Pope is forgiving the priests for having sex with children so it is no longer a so called Conspiracy Theory! It is a fact! However I challenge you to do some research yourselves, don't just take my word for it! Other Christian religions have been exposed for doing this also.

I have also found that my Narcissist was very good at having affairs, he tried so hard to make me jealous but it didn't work! In fact, the opposite was the case, every time he found someone new, it wasn't me he was bashing so I was extremely grateful! I learned to overcome jealousy with Rudy. I had been so jealous with him, he was always surrounded by other women it just ate away at me, it was horrible so I vowed and declared after Rudy left, that I would never do that again!

The Narcissist drop you when they realise you have been drained of your "Narcissistic supply" so they go looking for a fresh supply. Personally I observed they are always looking for their next "fix" of attention. Always on the "prowl", like a bee looking for new flowers to gather nectar from, sorry bees.

I would strongly suggest getting yourself tested for sexually transmitted diseases from this behaviour of theirs. Insist they use a condom with you is also a plan! Michael would use sex as a means of recovering from his hangovers, eventually I gathered enough courage to refuse to have sex with him.

I believe he was having other affairs before I refused to have sex with him. My daughter is a very powerful "Hollow Bone" and at five years old, she would channel Healing Energy for him which would dissolve his hangovers. I did not find this out until she told me many years later. Come to think of it, that probably had a lot to do with Anthony getting into trouble for things she did! Now it is very clear why he never got upset at her!

You need to understand Narcissists have NO EMPATHY! Everything is about them, they have such a massively distorted self-image, their egos are so huge it is a wonder they can walk through doorways figuratively speaking. They love using rage to manipulate and control. To have us Empaths cowering in fear gives them much delight, having us walk on eggshells, never knowing what is going to upset them next, is so emotionally and mentally draining for us! Totally exhausting in fact. Vanity, prestige and personal power are what they crave intensely, it must be all about them! They have absolutely no interest in attending to the needs of others who are totally invisible to them! You may say they don't give "two hoots" about anyone but themselves! They use rage in response to a perceived threat to their self-esteem or self-worth!

I found it very easy to be extremely critical of myself as many had been critical of me. We need to learn to be gentle with ourselves! It took many decades to learn how to be a Rescuer and be totally invisible to ourselves, due to be told on countless occasions that we didn't deserve. Therefore it became our reality thanks to the sub conscious failing to recognise the difference between Truth and a lie.

We need to learn to put down those clubs we keep beating ourselves over the head with and give ourselves permission to be the students of life that we are. In other words, we need to learn to be gentle with ourselves! Let us be real, it will take longer than a weekend working on ourselves for us to emotionally heal from all the emotional, mental and physical abuse we experienced. We are so good at bending over backwards for everyone else, time to do it for ourselves.

We cannot give to others from an empty cup. Doing our Emotional Healing work is like working down through the layers of an onion. Eventually we begin to fill our cups through doing nice things for ourselves, so they overflow and we can give to others without depleting ourselves! It is time to focus on what we want and need for ourselves, which is extremely challenging, as we are so good at being invisible to ourselves. Often we fail to recognise how our whole life has been focused on pleasing / appeasing the Narcissist, ignoring or outright denying our own needs. As a result of this we often find we either have no boundaries or very unhealthy ones at best.

Personally I went NO CONTACT once I left, a tactic I cannot recommend strongly enough! You need to realise they will NEVER change, never mind what they tell you, they tell the biggest lies out! Never contact them once you are away from them because they will beg you to come back saying how sorry they are and how they will never abuse you again. They will change for a couple of weeks if you are lucky then abuse you twice as bad as they did before because you dared to leave.

I saw it happen so many times when I was in Refuge. Personally I changed my phone number and email address. As my Narcissist was so in tune with my energy, even though he didn't believe he was psychic (walking towards me in a large department store four hours after I had left home) told me otherwise. I needed to change the vibration of my energy that I was sending out. That was a very effective blocker. A word to the wise, once you get onto Centrelink benefits, make sure your file is sealed so it requires two people to sign to gain access to your information. My Narcissist had contacts within the department and utilised their ability to access my file.

When I was in Refuge they did all the legal court stuff for me. He was granted Open Access at one stage but when the Court closed down and was amalgamated with a larger Court, the new Court could not find the paperwork granting him Open Access. I did not find this out for many years after the original Court case. Not quite sure how he pulled that one off, all I remember is standing outside the Court, his mother was with him. Of course he had her wrapped around his little finger. She was an alcoholic, like him, but he would bash her as well sadly.

Supervised access was an option I had back then and I took advantage of it so I didn't have to see him that way. He used this "Open Access Order" as an excuse to keep coming back to me every time one of his other relationships failed. I have no idea what happens now 40 years later, you will need to do your own research regarding that.

Sometimes when you leave in a hurry you may not have time to pack so make sure you keep your medications with you at all times! You can always buy clothes and toiletries once you are safe and I found that the Refuges had emergency clothes you could have if it was needed.

The most important thing is to GET OUT SAFELY! I strongly advise you plan your escape ahead but keep it to yourself! Children may not agree with you and tell the Narcissist! Many an Empathic Rescuer has been put in severe danger because their children contact the Narcissist, please be aware of this extreme danger and take appropriate steps to maintain your own safety. Their friends or relatives can be a safe haven for these children if necessary. It is a lot to weigh up and definitely not a decision you make lightly, but as I must insist, your safety, and even your life, may depend on this!

Narcissists can become extremely violent, these stories you hear about one spouse being killed, in my opinion, a Narcissist is involved, usually the murderer I would take a guess at. Occasionally the person being abused will snap and do some damage to the abuser. Please LEAVE before it gets to this point as it is the children that suffer or are also killed at times. Bitter custody battles leave the children very vulnerable. Courts need to be more aware of Narcissistic behaviour but then, how many of them are Psychopaths Sociopaths I would love to know. Anyway, this is just my opinion.

Once you are safe you can contact them to let them know you are safe, NOTHING ELSE! I was able to contact my parents and sister because they knew he was abusing me. Many times the Narcissist will turn your family and friends against you if he or she has been able to con them and make you out to be the bad person. Use your discernment when letting people know you are safe. If you are unsure whether they are being influenced by the Narcissist go no contact with them as well as it is a favourite ploy of the Narcissist to turn everyone against you! It is important for both their safety as well as yours that you go NO CONTACT with everyone the Narcissist knows.

Your workplace, any sports or hobbies the children have, will be the second place the Narcissist searches for you once they realise your friends and family truthfully have no idea where you are so be prepared for this! You will need to leave your job and the children will need to stop attending their sports / hobbies etc in the area they have been attending. Remember many sports are competitive so many clubs meet and the Narcissist will check them all out! As a result you will need to find new employment and the children will need to find new interests. Nowadays, a lot of children are on Social Media so that is a way they can be tracked also! You need to be very careful of the track ability of what you choose to do. The best idea is to make new friends and stay away from anyone who knows you from your old life as they are weak points that can leak information to the Narcissist. Remember one of the favourite tricks of a Narcissist is to turn everyone against you once you leave so it is best to give them a wide berth and just stay away.

As a Rescuer we never become visible to ourselves until we "Crash and Burn". When we only hurt a little bit, we lick our wounds for a few days then go back to being good little "doormats" because of our deep need to be needed! That is one of the main reasons we bring Narcissists into our lives, other than Karmic reasons, because sooner or later they will bring you to that point unless they kill you first! That depends on the experience you have chosen to have before you got here. We all have several "exit points" we can choose to take before the final one which is what happens in the case of suicides, they take an early exit point because staying to learn the lessons, they themselves chose on a Soul level, is too hard for them.

The "gift" Narcissists give us Rescuer/ Empaths is getting us to that point of "Crash and Burn" so we eventually become visible to ourselves so we can begin our Healing journey. Doing our Inner Child work and learning to RECEIVE instead of just giving.

Learning to ask for help is a massive lesson in itself because we are stubborn and independent and we don't need anybody! Our loved ones in Spirit, who have incarnated here, are the ones who help us with daily living problems because they have been here and they know how it works, our Guides / Guardian Angels help us with other things but none of them can help us until we ASK for their help! The way they help us is often having us in the right place at the right time, having thoughts coming back to us in answer to the question we asked or having things "jumping out" at us in the form of number plates, sign posts etc. As Spirit having a Human experience we need to learn, NOTHING is ever done to us! On a Soul level we create situations for our own Personal Growth and because we are imperfect we often have to repeat these lessons till we eventually learn it.

CHAPTER ELEVEN

My time in Refuge

It takes a lot of Courage to make the massive decision to leave your old life which has got far too dangerous and abusive for you to stay in. Not only for your own sake but for the sake of your children also! What we need to remember is that our children's "Love Equation" is formed during the first seven years of their life! We tend to repeat the same "Love Equation" that was given to us when we were children, with our own children because to us it is "normal" and everyone else is experiencing the same thing. Well, there is a Universal Law that says Like attracts Like, so when we are being abused, the people around us are also in abusive situations so that reinforces within us that abuse is "normal"

Mixed in with the Courage to leave the dangerous and abusive situation is a lot of FEAR, CONFUSION, DOUBT, GUILT and many other negative emotions. Some of us have our own homes, it takes a lot to walk away from that, I know, I did it! The Narcissist in my life thought he had me trapped, that I would no longer run away from him because I was buying my own home so the abuse was turned up a notch or two!! Having to take your children away from their friends, to attend new schools is a massive consideration but the worst case scenario if you don't do is that the Narcissist may actually murder you and then your children would have to live their lives without you to protect them.

The children may also be at risk of being murdered also. Yes, it is absolutely a massive decision to make to walk away, or in my case, run like the wind literally, the first time I escaped, and yes, ESCAPE is literally what we need to do for our own safety and that of our children! It is massively overwhelming, many Empath / Rescuers don't even have their own money or have any idea how to budget or pay bills as the Narcissist often has full control over the finances.

My parents were beautiful when it came to teaching us about how to handle money. We would get an allowance but we had to write down every time we spent money and what we spent it on. At the end of the week we had to add it up and see how much money we still had, if the account balanced, we then got our next week's pocket money! It was a powerful, extremely valuable tool and I am so Grateful to my parents for doing that with me. I believe these skills should be taught in schools under the class label of LIFE SKILLS! Many parents are very busy or are unable to teach their children for many different reasons so for it to be taught at school would be something all children would benefit from is my personal belief!. When I was at High School we did sewing, Cookery and Woodwork, I don't believe this is done in many schools today which is sad, having life skills is just so important!

When I went into Refuge there were no Counsellors available, when I earn lots of money from selling my book I would love to be able to rectify this situation as we go through a very deep Grieving process, we are mourning our past lives that have been so damaged. Someone doesn't have to die to grieve, having to walk away from the only life you have known to begin something very different that you have no idea how to do is massive and we need all the help we can get or we just go back into old behaviour patterns and repeat what we have just left. Feeling lonely and incomplete, half an apple is what I refer to it as, is an extremely dangerous space to be in because this emotional place is what opens the door wide to Narcissists to come into our lives so if we haven't done our Inner Child Work and heal the Abandonment/Abuse / Chaos equals Love, we just continue repeating the same pattern!

We need to become a mother, or in the case of Empathic / Rescuer males, father to our own Inner child. This is how we eventually bring Tender loving care into our lives as we learn to Nurture ourselves! We can then become whole apples all on our own, no more feeling empty and lonely, it doesn't matter if we are on our own, we can be happy and contented! We need to become caterpillars and go within our cacoons for a couple of years so we can transform ourselves from incomplete to complete! We need to be gentle with ourselves, chaos, abuse, abandonment has been our normal way of living for many decades, it is going to take longer than a year to heal all that damage! Learning how to receive is a massive challenge for us Rescuers, we are stubborn and have learned to rely upon only ourselves. The most frustrating thing for our Guardian Angels, Guides, Loved ones on the other side of life is their inability to assist us UNTIL WE ASK / PRAY for their assistance! The way they help us is by having us in the right place at the right time, having things jumping out to us or by having thoughts coming in answer to thoughts we send out! We can call this listening to our Intuition, our "Gut Feeling" It doesn't help us because we tend to be major "Control Freaks" and use our logical minds for things that aren't maths or science. The life decisions we make using our logical minds always fall apart!

Trust is a massive issue for us to the point we don't even trust the guidance we receive from our Guides. They might tell us one thing but we have already decided we want to do something us which is why we are so good at doing confusion. We need to ask for the guidance before we go to bed and have a pad or something we can put the answers into or onto as soon as we wake up before our logical mind takes us into massive confusion! Just a hint, the thing you are arguing against is probably the guidance your Guides have given you! Keeping in mind that we go by what we analyse as far as life is concerned, not maths or science, always falls apart on us. The massive challenge for us is to Surrender and Trust so we can go by what our Guides tell us, it always works out right! Not necessarily the way we thought we wanted it!

From my friends place I went into Refuge for the 3rd time in 17 years. First of all we went to a temporary weekend Refuge. The hardest part for me on the Monday was driving a long way to an area I didn't know to be met by a Worker from the next Refuge. I had to then follow her to the Refuge. It is always a learning curve sharing a house with other very stressed and traumatised strangers, one family to a room. There is a roster of chores that must be done including planning what food you are going to buy and cook for everyone. Thankfully the workers assist you with that job but it is up to you to prepare and cook the food for everyone! I have only ever had a small family so that was quite the learning curve. Trying to sleep in a strange place with your children or other people's children crying was quite a challenge also. Finding towels and sheets was quite challenging at times when there were a lot of families in there. Finding the washing machines empty so you could wash your clothes and hang them out to dry, hoping it wasn't going to rain. This Refuge was in amongst some hills so pushing prams up and down hills when you were tired and stressed was quite the challenge, never mind ice on the roads that made it especially slippery, very challenging indeed. We also had to contend with people who were sick, of course, we were all in close quarters so we would get sick as well. Babies and children coming in with conjunctivitis, would spread through the other kids like wildfire, yes there were indeed a lot of challenges living in such close quarters with absolute strangers who were also extremely traumatised. Sadly stealing sometimes occurred as well, not just the children, but the mothers as well, like we needed more stress on top of what we had already been through. The most important thing however was that we were safe from our abusive partners. Some women felt so overwhelmed being away from their partners they went back to them! Doing stunts like that could get you killed, seriously! It is a massive decision to leave an abusive relationship when they have you living in absolute fear for not only your safety but your children's safety also, it takes a massive amount of courage to do this. Once again, staying in that abusive relationship can get you severely emotionally and physically injured if not killed which has happens in instances you hear on the news sadly.

The hardest thing I found when I went into Refuge was that I couldn't tell my friends, family or the children's schools or my work where I was because the Monster / Narcissist would go to all these people to try and find me. When they can no longer control you the turn these people away from you if they can get away with it because to an outsider, they act so innocent like butter wouldn't melt in their mouths plus they are such smooth talkers and excellent liars. They have 2 personalities, one for people who don't know them and then when you are in a close relationship with them you see the evil, nasty side of them and nobody wants to believe you. They are brilliant con artists. I am very grateful my parents and my sister had him worked out. When you are in Refuge you go through a grieving period because you cannot contact your loved ones, for both your sake and theirs. They cannot have information squeezed out of them if they don't have any. Sadly several women contacted their abuses who promised to change, which they did for a couple of days then exhibited worse behaviour than before because you had dared to leave them! May I strongly suggest that you never believe their lies about them being willing to change, it won't get better, just worse! Of course the best thing is never ever contact them again, let the lawyers handle all that!

He had been a Private Detective so had found me even after I had been rehoused, he had contacts in Social Security who leaked my information to him. Yes, that is horrifying to think that your information can be leaked. Three weeks after we were relocated my son left home, his girlfriend, who was 15 years older than him was also passionate about Dr Who so manipulated him. Well it turned out that he had a Soul Contract with her to bring through 2 daughters, both of whom are autistic. Her eldest daughter is 3 years younger than his sister and she was pregnant with a son at the time so my son was the only father he knew. I learned years later my son was a very abusive father so his wife put their son into a boys' home rather than kicking my son out of the home for abusing her son. I need to remember that on a Soul level, her son chose to have that experience. I must admit, I was horrified when I heard about what had happened, that my son had taken after his father. He was such a beautiful child and we were very close until his future wife stepped in. His eldest stepdaughter also told me that my son's father had threatened to kill her mother as well, this seems to be a pattern of Michael, apparently. Her mother begged him to stop seeing his father but he refused to stop seeing him. Eventually she gave him an ultimatum that if he didn't stop seeing his father she would leave him! Apparently this was the impetus he needed to finally stop seeing his father. When I understood that my son was also a Narcissist that made sense to me why he didn't care that his father was threatening to kill his wife, never mind he had done the same to his mother! He didn't seem to see anything wrong with his father's behaviour sadly. I had to realise he was a Narcissist himself apparently! I asked a Medium to help me connect with Anthony, Christopher came through and told me he had pushed the personality that was Anthony right down, that he was trying to kill him because he was afraid that if Anthony got strong and came to the surface again that he, Christopher would cease to exist, and he was determined that Anthony would never come to the surface again. Anthony was such a beautiful caring child, he acted as a father figure to his sister and my Family Day Care kids. He was an Empathic Rescuer like myself. He was very Psychic, he was Clairvoyant, he could see Spirit, he was Clairaudient, he could hear Spirit like we can hear each other. He would communicate with his older brother Peter, who is in Spirit regularly. He would also do Automatic writing. As his father was a Catholic, he insisted that both the children went to Catholic schools. In year 10, Anthony chose to shut down. He used to get real cranky at me when I asked him if Peter was around, he would say to me, "Just open up!" I would ask him how do I do that? Sadly he could never explain to me what to do. Three years after he left home I caught up with him on a tram, he was a Tram Conductor out from the Glenhuntly Depot. I asked him if he still spoke to his brother, he admitted he had forgotten how to. At the time, the partner I had after his father had also been on the receiving end of Narcissistic abuse. He was also Psychic and would ask me why the No3 tram kept jumping out at him. I said to him, maybe because it runs past our front door! He was picking up on Anthony being a tram conductor, I never saw that coming! It proved his Psychic ability to me. I got the confirmation that Anthony was a Tram Conductor through the mother of one of the other children that also went to Saint Colmans in Balaclava. She asked me how my daughter liked going to Caulfield North, I looked at her in shock wondering how she knew my daughter went there as I hadn't seen her for years. She then proceeded to blow my mind severely by asking me how did my son like being a Tram Conductor. That was the answer I had been looking for so I raced home, got some photos of Anthony, went to school and picked my daughter up then went around to the Tram Depot. I asked to speak to someone in charge, explained to them I hadn't seen Anthony for three years and that his father had threatened to kill me and burn my home to the ground. He had left home three weeks after we had been relocated. I was told he was due to come into the Depot shortly and to sit in the tram stop across the road and he would call Anthony off the tram so I could see him. I was so shocked at what I saw, there was this very skinny kid, so unlike the chubby boy I knew. I found out the reason he had lost so much weight was because he had been diagnosed with Diabetes. Every little sniffle my children or the Family Day Care kids would have, I would take them to the doctor, Jessica Ho. She never diagnosed his Diabetes and we saw her for several years! I must admit I was furious when I found out that he was undiagnosed Diabetic. How could she not suspect this and test him for it? I was not a neglectful mother yet this made me feel like the worst mother in the world. Even now, after all these years, I am sitting here in tears writing this.

One of the times I escaped from the Narcissist in my life was when I was pregnant with my daughter. We had gone up to Jupiter's Casino on the Gold Coast, not long after it had opened. Michael had got into the Champagne Cocktails again and we had a massive argument where he threatened to kick me until I aborted my daughter. Previously I had promised him I would never take his son away from him again. He was 8 years old at the time. We were up in the room. I knew I had to escape but I kept my promise and left Anthony in the room for his father. The Salvation Army took care of me and got me back to Tramville. My daughter's father, David Humphreys, that I had met when I was 16 through John Broman who had been on a Camping trip with Dad, my sister and I to Tasmania, set me up in a flat in Murrumbeena. Of course I missed my son severely so went to his school. The Principle, Carmel Myers has been conned by Michael to let him know when I came to see Anthony, she got sucked in by his lies so called him. Once again, I had Michael back in my life.

Just a little side note here, it is my experience with clients that whatever I have experienced I draw people to me that are going through similar experiences. You cannot empathise with your clients unless you have gone down the same type of pathway they are going through but walking on eggshells for 17 years, never knowing what was going to send him into a rage next, is not something I would wish on anybody but the only persons lessons we can learn is our own! I found it very difficult watching my daughter experience a lot of the stuff I had gone through! She always prided herself on learning the lessons much faster than I did but she has 5 children who are learning Narcissistic behaviour as "normal" so they will either follow their father's role model and become Narcissists themselves or bring Narcissistic partners into their lives. I understand that on a Soul Level they chose this experience but I could no longer be in that energy so I had to step away and it has been challenging. I was very close to my daughter for many years, I use to believe we were joined at the hip so when I was told that we would experience a situation that would separate us I thought they were full of it and that they must have been wrong but I had to eat humble pie eventually and admit her prediction was in deed accurate and that experience totally blew my world apart. I love my daughter to Eternity and back but I cannot learn her lessons for her and that was a very challenging lesson for me as well because all you want to do with your children is wrap them in cotton wool and keep them safe; but that dis empowers them, and stops them from learning the lessons that on a Soul level, they have chosen to learn!

You see many of us are also Rescuers and so we bring "Poor me" victims into our lives. All we know to do is give, we have immense difficulty in receiving as we hold a deep seated belief that we don't deserve! That is why we only know how to give, as we feel unworthy to receive! Our victims are our form of distraction, we run around like headless chooks running around after everyone else so we don't have time to look at our own hurt and pain! We don't become visible to ourselves until we "crash and burn" and oh boy, the Narcissists in our lives certainly do that for us!

You see whatever we are given in the first 7 years of our lives is what we take on board as "Love". Us Rescuers often have Abandonment, Trauma, Drama, Chaos as our "Love Equation" Our parents may have fought a lot, we may have fought with siblings, our parents may have been workaholics, maybe they were unable to emotionally communicate or maybe only one parent was around. This then becomes our "normal" and when we get into relationships as adults, we often repeat our parent's patterns which has been passed down over many generations! and receiving help. We tend to be stubborn and independent, never being able to rely on the victims in our lives for support. They only know Service to Self, not Service to Others like we do.

The only way to stop this pattern is to do our "Inner Child" work. We have great difficulty in asking and receiving help. We tend to be stubborn and independent, never being able to rely on the victims in our lives for support, all they know how to do is take!

We need to become a parent to our own "Inner Child". Learning how to become visible to ourselves is so challenging!! Something we can do for ourselves is to look in the mirror every morning and tell our Inner Child how much we love them and we are sorry for neglecting them so badly but from today on wards we promise to nurture them. This can be as simple as doing creative things we use to do as a child such as drawing, painting, listening to or playing music. We might have enjoyed baking biscuits or cakes for fetes or fairs. Maybe playing in the garden, planting seeds, flowers, weeding the garden, growing our own vegetables etc. Cast your minds back, what put a smile on your face and your heart when you were a child? Maybe having an ice cream was a rare treat that you really enjoyed on special occasions. Making daisy chains, weaving with paper to make place mats, making paper hats. Perhaps these are some things you can do with your children or Grandchildren to get them away from their electronic games. Who remembers playing with a skipping rope or playing hopscotch? Riding our bikes was always fun. How about board games such as Twister or Monopoly? I know we use to enjoy playing card games as a family. Mum use to make a special fuss for whoever lost by giving them a boobie prize. Made losing a lot less painful that is for sure! Putting our hair in curlers was always a special treat, nowadays just playing with different ways to do your hair. Can you tell I had long hair? Lol So what I am saying is that there are a lot of things we can bring back from our childhood. I used to enjoy playing on the swings and the see-saws and getting dizzy on the round metal structures that had mesh between the spokes and you had a friend push it around for you, then you took turns being on it. Some parks still have swings, maybe you can still sit on the seat and have a swing while you go back in your memory to your childhood. Who enjoyed making sandcastles when they were at the beach? Sand sculpture is now a very refined art with competitions I understand. A bit more sophisticated than out sandcastles but maybe we can still do them with the kids and gather shells to decorate them with.

Looking back on my life I guess I can relate to some qualities that are attributed to Starseeds. The biggest one for me was that I was the "Black Sheep" of the family. I really felt like a square peg in a round hole like someone had dropped me off and forgotten to pick me up again. I truly felt like an outsider, big time! When I got older I had a friend tell me I was an Old Soul and that truly resonated with me. I felt I had blue skin, I had no idea why but I connected with a guy who worked with the Andromedians and I discovered why I felt I had blue skin. Robert told me he had never met an Andromedian with such bright blue skin as my mother, on one level that obviously had stuck with me. Would you be surprised if I told you blue is my favourite colour? Well at least, now I know why, lol. I believe my psychic abilities are strong due to being a Starseed. I began wondering as I got older, why am I here? I came to the conclusion that I must have something pretty important to achieve but I had no idea what that looked like just that I had a deep need to be of Service to others which is why I became a Counsellor. I had to use my psychic gift in doing this work however. Being a Loner basically all my life has now changed as I have connected to likeminded people who see the world as I do. I am not as Empathic as some people but dogs, babies and little children seem to get drawn to me. Some Empaths are so sensitive they cannot cope in crowded places, I am glad crowded places do not affect me. To me, Spirituality sits far better with me than the manipulation and control of Religion, but each to their own. As a Spiritualist I totally respect the pathway each person is on to learn the lessons they have chosen, I see Earth as a School of Life where nothing is ever done TO YOU, rather it is created by you for your own personal growth. When I use to catch the bus to work or I was on the train, it wasn't unusual for total strangers to open up to me and share their worries or life stories with me. These are my experiences, may I suggest you do some research to identify other Starseed traits.

I grew up a Catholic like my father, my mother belonged to the Church of Christ. I grew up during the war in Ireland between the Catholics and protestants. In those days, when I was at primary school, the Catholics and protestants would throw stones at each other. I have been a "Loner" most of my life and I believe this played a large part in this. I do remember being at kindergarten and nobody playing with me. Mum did explain to me I didn't start kindergarten until 3rd term. I was born with Talipes, my feet were twisted inwards so I wore calipers up till I began school so that is another factor that came into play making me a loner. I was a catholic that had been raised in a State School and went to mass every Sunday to hear it in Latin which of course I didn't understand but I learnt all the responses! When I went to High School Latin was offered but that was for the kids who wanted to become doctors and that wasn't me so I learnt French.

It came in handy when I went to New Zealand and worked at the Rawhiti Trust Private Hospital in Mount Eden, Auckland. I could see One Tree Hill from outside my room window, the tree was actually still there then. Anyway, a lot of our clients there were rich Tahitians who spoke French! The Tahitians would gift us with shell necklaces when they left the hospital to all those who took care of them. I was the only non-Tahitian who got to go to dinner with them before they went back home, such a beautiful memory. They would insist that we left the classroom during religious instruction so that made my sister and I "outsiders" at school.

The day I was born, after my mother had gone through 3 days of Labour, I decided that I had changed my mind, I did no longer want to be here. My entrance had been very harsh, I feel so deeply for my mother once I had children of my own! I tried to exit stage left, my father had a mass said for me and I came back. It wasn't the mass that brought me back, it was the reminder that I received from my Guides that I had chosen, volunteered even, for this mission. I was reminded I had a "contract" to full fill. This was a very important time in history to incarnate, many had volunteered but few were chosen. I had been given a very important role to complete, Mother Earth and Humanity were going to experience massive changes and I was part of the Team that would assist in this process, as are all Starseeds incarnated now! This time, we are going to be successful Ascending into the 5th Dimension!

Let me share with you also, I was the result of a one night stand! The effort I went to to get my parents together especially as my father was engaged to be married to a good little catholic girl. Just what my Nana wanted for him but it was not to be. By the way everyone, as Spirit, we DO CHOOSE OUR PARENTS! We have often Reincarnated with them in Past Life, just playing different roles like your father may have been your sister or your child in Past Lives if they are a part of our Over soul Group. Have you ever met someone for the first time in this lifetime and felt like you have known them for a few thousand years, that is because you have had many reincarnations with them and on a Soul level, you know each other very well indeed! You have played many different roles with them over many, many Lifetimes! They don't need to have been your husband or wife or Lover in Past Lives, they may have been a neighbour, a friend etc. I apologise if I have just spun you out severely but hasn't these connections with total strangers in this life been really playing on your mind trying to figure how on earth you feel so deeply connected to them?

CHAPTER TWELVE

Relationship Patterns

Our "Love Equation" comes from the first 7 years of our lives. If there is constant arguing in our household, either between our parents or with our siblings, then Chaos and Drama will play a major part in our adult relationships. If our parents are workaholics, not physically around as in single parent families or are unable to emotionally communicate, then Abandonment becomes our Love Equation. Some of us developed a "I don't deserve" belief system so we become Rescuers who have an A plus in giving and a Z minus in receiving. We tend to be very good at being invisible to ourselves, putting everyone else first and ourselves last. One of the main things us Rescuers need to learn is a magical word called NO, which we need to invent for ourselves as it fails to be a part of our vocabulary. We need to create boundaries to stop being there for adults who are never there for us and we need to learn how to do nice things for ourselves. This is extremely challenging for us as we only feel comfortable in giving. Healing our Inner Child is a very slow lengthy process. We often feel we take three steps forward and two steps back, we just need to continue doing those 3 steps forwards!

In my case I have experienced Abandonment in my life over many Past Lives so it is not only what you experience in this life that affects you. I have found Energy Healing to be very effective in dealing with this situation as it has a very long "taproot" into many Past Lives.

Energy Healers clear energies out of our Auras before they manifest into our physical bodies. For issues that have already manifested into our physical bodies it is one of the tools we can use to release them as we need to heal on the Mental, Emotional, Spiritual and Physical levels. This Healing is like an onion, it has many layers until we finally reach the centre core issue so we may feel we have already addressed many of the issues. We just deal with thin layers in an attempt to prevent ourselves going into overwhelm. This tends to get quite frustrating for many of us because we believe we have already addressed that particular issue. What we need to remember is that we are going down to the next layer, baby steps are very important.

Until us Rescuers learn to become visible to ourselves and Rescue US, who is the only person we can truly Rescue, Victims are just our distractions to stop us looking at our own stuff, we keep bringing Victims into our lives.

When we feel lonely on our own it is a good indication that we are "Half Apples" looking for someone outside ourselves to make us feel whole and complete. Two half apples make a very dysfunctional relationship!

The best relationship we can have is when we feel whole and complete on our own and we no longer have that aching "need" to have someone in our lives to make us feel complete. As there is a Law that states," Like attracts Like", when we feel whole and complete on our own, then we attract a partner who is also whole and complete. This does not mean we will stop presenting ourselves with lessons to learn for our own personal growth, it just means we will view them as a learning curve instead of something bad that someone did to us.

We are able to gauge where we are on our Healing path by the people who surround us. If they are still doing "Poor me and Blame" then we know we are still playing Rescuer. If we find ourselves stressing or worrying about situations (God's job) or other adults behaviours (Their responsibility) then there is quite a big possibility we are still in Rescuer mode. If we find ourselves surrounded by people who are there for us as much as we are there for them then there is a rather large possibility that we have learnt to rescue ourselves! Congratulations job well done!

I have been inspired to speak about the main relationships I have chosen in this life. I believe we choose relationships as a part of our Soul Contracts, for me it is all about lessons and tying up loose ends on a Karmic level. Once again I would like to share my belief that NOTHING in this life is EVER done to us! We create lessons so we can grow and this very much includes the relationships we choose to experience.

The first one I would like to share with you is my daughter's father whom I met when I was 16. I will always remember the inner Knowing I had that I was going to have a daughter with him and at that stage I was totally unaware of my Psychic abilities, I was a good little catholic girl! Well, 16 years later I reconnected with him through friends. The first time we made Love and I didn't fall pregnant I remember thinking that something wasn't quite right. The second time we connected I fell pregnant and everything was all right with the world! It was such a smooth pregnancy compared to my two sons.

After David was taken out of my life when I was 16, it was a long distance relationship (Abandonment, Chaos, Drama was the Love Equation I created, along with massive Control as my parents were extremely strict!)

My next main relationship was with a beautiful Scottish young man, we both shared deep generational skeletons in our closets. He moved and I lost contact with him, we were both still at Secondary School into the higher Forms. I found out 15 years later that he had passed over in a motor bike accident as he came through at Church with Evidence of Survival. He has been with me ever since he passed over, in fact he took care of my eldest son when he passed over.

I have had him walking by my side ever since he crossed. He has told me I taught him about Love as our connection is extremely powerful to the point of my daughter falling pregnant and I told her that her son's name was Billy. Apparently Billy made a contract with this Soul to allow him to come through and spend time with me. As a result Cooper does not know me because Billy would come and spend time with me through Cooper's body. Billy did some further training and is now one of Cooper's Guides. I am very pleased Billy did this as Cooper has difficulty in speaking, his tongue and brain don't cooperate very well so he has needed to go to a special school set up to support children with this condition.

My next main relationship was with Rudy, Peter's father. I was engaged to him for 2 years before jealousy and possessiveness on my part tore us apart. I felt like such a major failure as most other girls of my age were getting married.

This sent me into a major depression as well as grieving for my son.

I believe that before we Incarnate onto this Planet, we choose how many children we are having, we know what sex they are, whether we are going to raise them or somebody else and what side of life they choose to be on depending on what lessons they choose to learn. Peter chose to grow up on the other side, he is one of my daughter's Guides. I didn't understand this at that time. I know there are many people grieving the loss of their children. I just need to let you know that you raise them when you are asleep instead of when you are awake. Have you ever experienced putting something down then coming back like five minutes later and it isn't there? That is our Spirit Children playing with us, we just need to ask them to please bring the object back. They are just letting us know they haven't left us, they are closer than our own breath and that goes for anyone who has passed over that we are close to. They stay with us and walk by our sides, there is no such thing as time in Spirit, only down here in the Third Dimension.

The most frustrating thing for our Loved ones to witness is when we have a problem but we don't ask them for help. They know what it is like to be here so totally understand what it is like to deal with life down here. Their hands are tied until we ask for the help, us Rescuers tend to have major difficulty in doing that as we are so stubborn and independent, we don't need anyone or so we like to think. That is mainly because we surround ourselves with Victims because we have this deep need to be needed due to this Belief we have taken on board that states we don't deserve! This is why we only feel comfortable with giving. The people we give to tend to be Victims who only know how to take! A very unbalanced energy indeed! The Victims are our form of avoidance as they keep us running around like headless chooks!

My next major relationship was after I came back from 6 months overseas. Michael was a porter at the hospital where I worked. I was still feeling like a failure in my last relationship so when he began showing interest in me I got really excited. What I didn't understand at that time was that I am an Empath and Michael is a Narcissist. It is a situation many of us Empaths / Rescuers create in order to become visible to ourselves! In the beginning the Narcissist builds you up and puts you up on a pedestal. Once you feel comfortable up there they then begin criticising you for the very things they would praise you for in the beginning. This does our heads in severely so we go to extraordinary lengths to get back into their good books, not understanding what we did wrong. We get emotionally and physically abused. These Narcissists have a boundary around them. People on the outside of that circle think butter wouldn't melt in their mouths but once you cross that line and get close to them they become Jeckle and Hyde personalities. When we try to tell people what they are doing to us, the people on the outside don't believe us and tell us we are lying. It took me 17 years to finally escape him, third time lucky. He had a Private Investigators License so was able to access my Centrelink information. They have the "gift of the gab", telling everyone different stories. When they can no longer control you they turn your family and friends against you.

My next relationship came into my life when my daughter was 9 years old. His name was Theo. He had 3 sons which for a year would come and spend the weekend with us. Theo had also been on the receiving end of a Narcissist. He was psychic also. That is what attracted me to him. The Easter the year after we met, his ex took his sons to live in Queensland. Theo was a part of our lives till after my daughter had her first son and we moved to Queensland after holidaying up on the Gold Coast at the fun Parks. We were on our way home and I said to her that I belonged in Queensland. I told Theo I was coming up here to meet the man I was meant to be with. I could tell him that as we were both Psychic. It took a few years before I met that man, in the meanwhile Theo tried to come back into my life by inviting himself up here which went down like a lead balloon! He was so desperate to stay with us that he stashed his driver's license and his other ID in the back of a drawer which we found when we moved! I dropped him at the airport and he rang me to say he couldn't find his ID so I told him they would allow him to get back on the plane as he had flown up here with it. My daughter would spend time with him when she went down to Tramville. He had been the male role model as she was growing up. He had stored a lot of the stuff we were unable to bring up to Queensland so after I met Gunter I went down to Tramville with my daughter and her two youngest children to sort my stuff out.

Gunter is Psychic as well. We had only been at Theo's place for 5 minutes and my phone rang, it was Gunter telling me to get out of there now! I told him I was trying to sort stuff out and he told me to leave it there as I hadn't needed it since I had been up in Queensland. So Theo got to hear Gunter speaking with me which confirmed to him that I had indeed moved on! The timing of Gunter's call really blew both my daughter and myself away! Gunter knew Theo wanted me back in his life which is why he told me to get out of there!

Well, on the 4th July this year Gunter and I have been in each other's lives for 10 years. I have walked away from him several times but he loves fishing and keeps hooking me on his line and pulling me back in. I have come to understand the very deep Soul connection we have between us. On a Soul level we have known each other for aeons! I actually asked him tonight when we were on our nightly phone call how long he felt we had known each other for? Was it 10 years or much, much longer? His response, he didn't want to talk about it! All I wanted was to be with another Starseed who would understand me. He is still working on the understanding me part as he is just now understanding that if we have known each other on a Soul level for aeons, that he is also Pleiadian, which I had confirmed a couple of weeks ago by a lady who did a Past Life reading on our connection.

I have planted the seed in his mind now and I know it is growing as much as he would like to be in denial about it. These next few months will be very interesting as he wrestles with what he knows to be true but definitely does not want to know about it as it means that all I have been telling him is true and that will totally blow his mind!

I had been a basket case for 3 years after my son left home at 16 due to the influence of a lady 15 years older than him who had a daughter who was 3 years younger than his sister! On a Soul level, I had asked my son to teach me that we didn't own our children which was very hard for me because I felt "owned" by my mother until the day she died. Dad was the disciplinarian, using a strap and electric cord which was a step down from the horse whip that was used to discipline him. I feared my father, so never seemed to have got emotionally close to him like my sister was. My son married this woman when he was 18 and had two autistic daughters with her.

Us Rescuers have such a deep "I don't deserve" belief system that when we only hurt a little bit, we lick our wounds for a few days then go back to being doormats. In order for us to become visible to ourselves we need to "Crash and Burn". On a Soul Level this is the role we ask our Narcissists to play. Once we become visible to ourselves we can then begin healing our Inner Child by becoming parents to ourselves. Through becoming visible to ourselves we then are able to give ourselves Tender Loving Care and Support to ourselves and learn how to receive!!! I believe many of us Starseeds are tying up loose ends from Past Life relationships.

When we "Crash and Burn" and begin our Emotional Healing journey and raise our vibrations then gradually we will find we are able to release people and situations that no longer resonate with us and we connect with new people who are also working on themselves. There is a saying that says like attracts like and that goes for us raising our vibrations. Lower vibration people feel uncomfortable around our energies so choose to leave.

I am finding through the Counselling I am doing with my Readings, I am finding many of us Starseeds are now connecting with new partners or old partners are becoming "new" by working on themselves. We needed to heal ourselves and become "whole apples" all on our own rather than expecting someone else to make us feel whole and complete. I refer to that situation as being half an apple. We are often in full on Rescue mode when we feel this way. We need to learn the only person we can Rescue is ourselves!

CHAPTER THIRTEEN

Recognising we are Starseeds

How many of you feel like you were dropped off and they forgot to come and pick you back up again? I often felt this way, out of place here, like I simply didn't belong. How many of you can resonate with this feeling? Do you find yourself looking up at the stars and missing home but knowing where "home" is? Are you a loner feeling like a square peg in a round hole, like you just don't belong here?

There are several videos on You Tube which give you information on the Traits of Starseeds. This is one of them. Are You a Starseed? ~ Best 27 Characteristics That Will Give You The Answer! There is an interesting book written by Jo Amidon called "Where are You really from?" There is also a short video that uses that book as its basis What is Your Galactic Origin - Pleiades, Sirius, Andromeda, and More 107,834 views.

What I am sharing I hope will resonate with you so you know you are not alone. Yes, us Starseeds have been scattered far and wide! This causes us to feel so alone as we had no contact with other members of our Star Family. At last we have discovered there are many of us and that has been a massive relief, especially for us "First Wavers" as Dolores Cannon referred to us as!

Thank goodness for social media. It has enabled us Starseeds to find each other! We have been able to connect with Soul Family, Star Family, it has been so amazing, giving me immense joy connecting with likeminded people. People who understand us. Thank you Facebook! You never saw this coming did you! I have connected with beautiful people like David Icke who have taken us way down the "rabbit hole" and shared vital information with us, assisting us to see the truth of what is happening underneath the surface that the Illuminati / Cabal / Luciferians / Satanists, are doing. Very dark Agendas indeed! Thank you David, you are such a Blessing, sharing your vital hidden information with us! Allowing us to open our minds to the Truth of what is going on underneath the surface!

Face Book was created to obtain our personal information, sadly they do use information gathered from us to target us with adverts, but we don't have to buy anything unless we choose to.

For me, I have used Face Book to share knowledge, "plant seeds" to open people's minds. To awaken them to what is happening in this world underneath the surface such as do you realise many of the people in power, especially in America are SELECTED by the Illuminati / Cabal, not elected by the people! Massive shock hey! Many of these Illuminati / Cabal are in positions of power and immense wealth, they are the "Puppet Masters" of the people in power. One family you may have heard of are the Rothchilds, an extremely powerful family indeed!! Do your own research everyone!! Check out what the Reserve Bank really is and who our "Straw Person" is. An artificially created person by law at the time of your birth, the inscription of an ALL CAPITAL LETTERS NAME on your birth certificate / document which is a document of life and a negotiable instrument.

Do you believe humans are the only species in the whole of the Universes and Galaxies or does that sound totally unrealistic to you? The human mind has a tendency to think other life forms must be like us, three dimensional but what if there are higher vibrations and other beings are invisible to us or appear as orbs. Maybe they look different to us and are not humanoid like us, that is a mind expanding thought! Have any of you seen bright lights in the sky moving really fast changing directions that no plane is capable of doing? Maybe these bright lights have become very large and then totally disappeared. Maybe they have appeared out of nowhere (another dimension perhaps) and then disappeared after being visible for a short time travelling at speeds no jet can achieve. Have you ever seen extremely bright sparkling objects, much brighter than the surrounding stars that remain stationary but change in level of brightness?

Maybe they have been more than one colour like white, green and red or a single colour like bright green which has been so bright you have been able to get a photo of it at night-time? I have! They sparkle / twinkle so intensely they make the other stars look pale in comparison. I know they are not satellites because they are stationary! I see these two objects from my bedroom window. I do regular Night Watches looking for Craft / Ships / UFO's so have had a lot of experience in distinguishing the difference between these and stars / planets.

Over the past few years I have taken part in many Night Watches, mostly with a beautiful lady Lauren who is extremely in tune with the Ships and ET's, herself! She was able to feel their energy and using a laser light direct us towards where the ships were. She would also get us to focus on a particular area of the sky and sure enough, within a few minutes we would see a Ship appear in that area. She also used Crystal Bowls and Light Language to raise the vibrations to increase the connection with our Sky Family. She is an amazing facilitator and I am looking forward to doing many more Night Watches with her.

Recently I have connected with my Twin Flame, who naturally

is also a Starseed. Since we have connected we have been aware of a Golden Rectangular Ship making itself known to us, it allows me to video it on my 4G phone even when it is directly above our heads! It either keeps us awake or wakes us up. Once we go outside and acknowledge it, then we can go to sleep!

Recently, around my daughter's 33rd birthday, another Golden Ship made itself known to us! This one was a triangular shape and unlike the rectangular Golden Ship, it appears around 4am, quite close to the tree tops. It was extremely bright and interestingly, it didn't want to be photographed or videoed.

I had to speak with them in Light Language and try three times before they appeared, quite faintly, on my phone video, unlike the rectangular Ship which appears as a brilliant white spot. When I went out an hour later it was still at the same height but much further away horizontally. I am so pleased I had my Twin Flame as a witness to this!

He has been aware of the Ships since he was a child and can ask them not only to "Power up", which I can do as well, but to dance for him! They will do all these zig zag moves for him! I am yet to ask them to do this for me. I am thrilled enough when they "Power up" for me.

I have also been videoing the Golden rectangular ship while it has cloaked(disappeared), reappeared and then "Powered up", several times in a row! I feel very Blessed.

I will often wake up with various scratches, bruises, blisters (okay, the red marks were there when I woke up, the blisters took a couple of days to appear and got quite large).

One of them even got infected! I went to my doctor who sent a sample off to identify which organism created the infection, which you do. When he got the results back they could not identify the organism which created the infection! To me, that was proof that it was not originating from the Earth Plane!

The most recent experience I have had was waking up with several different splotches on blood near the hem of my nightie on the front of it! Now there was no smudging and there was no blood stains on my sheet either so the blood had totally dried by the time I got back here!

This reminds me of the time when I first arrived in Couldville in 2011. Within the first week of arriving there I woke up rubbing my hip! I was laying on my side. My first thought was, "Why am I rubbing my hip?". This was shortly followed by the realisation that my hip was rough! That really woke me up and aroused my curiosity massively! I got out of bed and walked to the mirror. I had to turn like 45 degrees to see three puncture marks, evenly spaced, vertically! The reason why it was rough was because the serous fluid had coagulated around the top of the holes! You bet I got some witnesses to see what had happened to my hip! It took me a day or so to realise there was absolutely NO PAIN! I would never have discovered them if I had not been rubbing my hip! It took me a while to realise wherever this happened, there was no gravity, otherwise it would have run down my hip instead of coagulating around the holes!

My girlfriend, Tina, in Couldville, that I met in 2012 when I was there, is extremely psychic herself. She has told me she has never seen anyone with as many Hybrid children as myself and my daughter have!

When I have my Energy Healing with a beautiful lady, Rita, my Pleiadian Family come into the Healing room. It really spun her out! She had never dealt with Galactics before! My friend Loraine was grounded so severely the first time she came with me the only thing she could move was her mouth. She kept yelling about green laser beams shooting through me! Although she is Clairvoyant, she had never dealt with Galactics either!

That Healing session I felt like I was in an operating Theatre with a lot of ET observers like in a room above the area I was in, with large glass windows so they could observe and learn from what was being done with me. I felt very calm and safe, I have absolute, and total trust, in my Sky Family and the Mantid Beings who work on me alongside my Pleiadian Family!

When Loraine would come with me I would have my session first after experiencing missing time on the way home the first time she was with me. She had her session first. I needed grounding severely as I felt I was half hanging out of my body, very lightheaded! I remember turning right onto the main highway. The next thing I know I am several minutes down the road and wondering how I got there!

Loraine said she went to speak to me, she turned around, the car was full of ET Beings and I was not there! The ET's had taken over my body and were driving the car using my body! Loraine was rather concerned when she realised I wasn't in my body but I know I am well looked after by my Sky Family so I was not in the least concerned when I realised I had experienced missing time while I had been driving.

After that session Rita got me to write the information I was given so I shall share it with you.

Love is all there is, let go of judgement, allow Peace and Harmony. Raise your vibration. Speak your Truth without harshness, be gentle in all that you do. Treat others the way you would like to be treated. Release negative energy, it does not serve you. Think three things before you speak, is it kind, is it truthful, is it necessary? Nurture yourself, put yourself first, you cannot give from an empty cup!

This is necessary so we can be of Service to others. When the glass is only half full you cannot be of Service to the best of your ability! When you constantly recharge yourself, the glass remains full, and this is the best space for you to be in to be of Service to others!

Ground, bare feet on Mother Earth is very nurturing for you. Learn to protect yourself from the negative energy of others. Tigers Eye, smoky quartz and Tourmaline are very good for protecting yourself. It is very important to prevent your energy from being drained.

Always ask for help and guidance from your Higher Self, Guides and loved ones who have passed over. Your loved ones are the best ones to assist you with your everyday issues as they know what it is like to live on this Earth Plane and the challenges we face, remember, they cannot assist you unless you ask for their assistance otherwise they are forbidden to interfere with your free will.

For Higher Spiritual knowledge ask your Higher Self, Guides and Sky Family. There are ready to work with you as soon as you request their assistance.

Some dreams may give insights into what is happening and why. Remember, this is a School of Life and as such nothing is ever done to us! They are all lessons that we ourselves, on a Soul level, create for our own personal growth! As we are imperfect, otherwise we would not need to be here in this school of life, we often have to repeat lessons many times before we finally learn them! Patience, tolerance, trust, forgiveness and acceptance are very good examples of this! The need to release judgement, not only of others but of ourselves also is a sneaky lesson.

When we incarnate we go through the grey mists of forgetfulness so we don't remember the lessons we have incarnated to learn. If we did, we would live a very unbalanced life just focusing on maybe one or two lessons. Many of them are intertwined so they are un-separable!

Some people choose to incarnate with disabilities, they sacrifice their lives and their own lessons in order to give others the opportunity to be of Service to them.

Rita got me to write this as soon as I was fully back in my body as she wanted an English translation of my Light Language.

The first time I experienced missing time I was with my daughter. We had been having this heated discussion about UFO's, she is very sceptical but my eldest grandson "knows" he is not from here, just like his Grandma! Anyway, we were sitting at the traffic lights and there was a mini minor in front of us converted into a Panel Van with a small ladder on the roof. We were discussing how they could possibly fit a toolbox into the back of it, it must have been a really tight fit or a very small toolbox!

Next thing we know we are twenty minutes down the road in

heavy traffic. It was my Grandson that came back first and asked how the mini had managed to get ten cars in front of us. I was shocked, I mentioned to my daughter that I had been unaware of the lights changing. The biggest surprise was, neither had she been aware of the lights changing, and she was driving! I guess Sky Family were just proving to her they were very real indeed! Mind you, there were quite a few traffic lights between where we had last been aware and where we found ourselves! This freaked her out so badly that within a month she had buried it so deeply that she could not remember the incident! Chris remembered it vividly however. Cognitive dissonance can affect us in many ways, giving us blackouts, burying memories that we cannot explain, is one way it works.

Personally I was very reluctant to come this time around. After my mother was in labour for 36 hours I tried to exit stage left but got sent back down here after being reminded I had a contract to fulfil.

Not happy I can tell you! I had a lot of karma from past lives to complete and believe me, that was a rough ride.

Some of you Empaths may have also had the challenging experience of bringing a Narcissist into your lives making your lives hell on Earth, it is a karmic experience. Narcissists place us on a pedestal and when we feel happy and comfortable they proceed to destroy us emotionally, nothing we do is good enough, and we are often physically abused as well. They threaten to kill us, in my case, if we leave. When we do escape, they turn our friends and family against us. You see, they have a dotted line around them, people on the outside of that dotted line think butter wouldn't melt in their mouths but once you are on the inside of that dotted line, it is like Jeckel and Hyde, man you see a very ugly side of them but nobody believes you! You see many of us are also Rescuers and so we bring "Poor me" victims into our lives. All we know to do is give, we have immense difficulty in receiving as we hold a deep seated belief that we don't deserve! That is why we only know how to give, as we feel unworthy to receive! Our victims are our form of distraction, we run around like headless chooks running around after everyone else so we don't have time to look at our own hurt and pain! We don't become visible to ourselves until we "crash and burn" and oh boy, the Narcissists in our lives certainly do that for us!

You see whatever we are given in the first 7 years of our lives is what we take on board as "Love". Us Rescuers often have Abandonment, Trauma, Drama, Chaos as our "Love Equation" Our parents may have fought a lot, we may have fought with siblings, our parents may have been workaholics, maybe they were unable to emotionally communicate or maybe only one parent was around. This then becomes our "normal" and when we get into relationships as adults, we often repeat our parent's patterns which has been passed down over many generations! and receiving help. We tend to be stubborn and independent, never being able to rely on the victims in our lives for support, all they know how to do.

The only way to stop this pattern is to do our "Inner Child" work. We have great difficulty in asking and receiving help. We tend to be stubborn and independent, never being able to rely on the victims in our lives for support, all they know how to do is take!

We need to become a parent to our own "Inner Child". Learning how to become visible to ourselves is so challenging!! Something we can do for ourselves is to look in the mirror every morning and tell our Inner Child that we love them! It can take a very long time for some of us to get to be able to look in that mirror! We need to heal on all levels, physical, emotional, mental and spiritual. In many cases it takes us decades to reach a point of being in enough pain for us to reach the point of "What about me??? I deserve better!" It is like, "Who is the I who deserves better?" We are extremely good at invisibility, putting everyone else first and ourselves last!

One tool I have found very useful in learning how to nurture ourselves is to get an exercise book and every time we do something nice for ourselves we write down the date, what it was we did, which could be as simple as spending time in nature, listening to music, doing something creative, it doesn't have to cost heaps of money and then giving ourselves a huge tick! Remember when you were in

Primary School and you got a maths sum right, how good that tick made you feel?

I am a "First Waver" as Dolores Cannon refers to us. She has some very interesting information, talking about first, second and third wavers coming here to Earth. There are many YouTube videos talking about Dolores Cannon and the Healing work she does. Please feel free to watch several to gain a deeper understanding of what she has done and the legacy she has left us!

Please feel free to do research on Starseed traits. Personally I relate to some of the traits they mention, not all of them. Due to us experiencing many lives on different planets that is why we will find there will be one Race that you resonate most strongly with but you will also have characteristics from other Races also!

I am an Empath, thankfully I don't have any issues in crowded places but dogs and small children tend to connect with me. Hold onto your hats, we are about to dive into the "Rabbit Hole" of where could you have come from before you came to Earth.

Some of the Planets you may have come from, and you have more than likely experienced life on several different ones, I know I have, are Pleiades, Sirius, Arcturus, Andromeda, Orion, Lyra and the list goes on! There are several videos explaining various traits of different Planets. Personally I didn't relate to some of the traits of the Planets I believe I have experienced but keep an open mind. That is an excellent suggestion when you are diving down into the extreme unknown and taboo subject of Aliens / Extra Terrestrials.

In Russia, the top ten Smerch Agents were supplied with a book on various Alien Species and they constantly update it. I found this very interesting video on You Tube called the 58 Races of the Russian Alien Races Book AZAZEL 8867. The book was found in the Grandfather's shed of one of Dante Santori's friends named Pedro. The Grandfather had apparently asked the boys to clear the shed out for him, he had totally forgotten about the book which was of course absolute top secret information for only the eyes of the top 10 people in Russia! Sadly Pedro was killed in a car accident which is why Dante chose to release this top secret information.

[Leaked] Russian Alien Races Book Dante Santori. This is the video you need to look for.

There are several other videos describing ET / Alien Races as well, here are a couple for you to check out for yourself : THE STAR RACES – TRAILER. These Are The 13 known Extraterrestrial Races Living On Earth.

David Icke 2018 ☯ Unmissable!!!! 29,863 views. Just had to include one of David's videos!

Now believe me or not, the Russian Government isn't the only Government with information on Alien / ET Species! If you listen to David Icke he will tell you some very juicy information and if I remember correctly some juicy tit bits are that the Black Ops Military actually work with the Greys in underground Military Bases in places such as Dulce, New Mexico. David shares that the Black Ops Military have advanced weaponry, trains that hover above a single rail and can go from America to the Australian Pine Gap American run Military Base in a couple of hours but they are not sharing this technology with the rest of us!

I have watched many videos regarding hidden information such as Phillip Schneider, interviews with Kerry Cassidy, interviews with Simon Parkes, an ex British Minister.

Free Energy that Tesla brought through is part of the advanced technology Benevolent ET's have shared with us but of course the oil / petroleum and electricity companies don't want this information being released of course! David will take you way down the rabbit hole but your mind needs to be like a functional parachute, OPEN! I would highly recommend to those of you with a thirst for the TRUTH and open minds, listen to David Icke's videos. He has written several books as well.

If I remember correctly, Operation Blue Book was set up to discredit people who saw UFO's or who were even abducted by them such as Betty and Barney Hill. In my understanding the Government have gone out of their way to cover up the reality of UFO's while secretly the Black Military Ops actually work with them. You wonder where Trillions of dollars have disappeared I suggest looking here may "find" the missing money! David Icke thinks so also! Totally makes sense to me! Once again, please understand this is my opinion.

I understand Experiencers / Contactees are often along a family line. I consider myself a volunteer Contactee as I have been told I have many Hybrid kids on the Craft as does my daughter. I resonate with this because I have been aware of feeling pregnant but I lose the child several times. I believe that before I incarnated here I chose to assist these dying Races, which I believe are us in the future.

From what I understand Artificial Intelligence made us part Human and part machine and eventually we were unable to reproduce.

I believe there are several different types of Greys, some are basically machines (the small ones I believe). I have also been led to understand that some of the Higher Dimensional ET's who have no body, use these Grey suits to exist on these lower dimensions so you never know who the occupants of these suits are.

When I went to Couldville I met a Cherokee Medicine Woman who remembered her child being taken from her on board the Craft and she was very upset about it but these children cannot exist here on Earth as they are more ET than Human. I do believe there are Hybrid children walking upon this Earth who are more Human than ET. They look so much like us except perhaps for small differences like pointed ears.

There was a Geologist, involved in building these DUMBS (Deep Underground Military Bases) that came across a nest of greys and was lucky to escape with his life, only that a Green Beret pushed him into the cage and sent him to the surface and died himself during the conflict. Phillip Schneider is his name. He even gave lectures and spoke of this incident. He lost parts of his fingers and toes from the blue lazer beam used by the Greys. As happens to many who speak out about the Truth, he was eventually murdered although the press claimed it was suicide.

In October 2017 I went to a Star Knowledge Conference in Tugun. Tolec, Adona and Alexandra Meadors from America were some of the Guest speakers. Adona runs a website called Star Ancestry. Anyway I really wanted to know what Galactic Heritage she would bring forward as I believe I have experienced lifetimes on many different planets such as Andromeda, this knowledge came from Robert Lomax.

Adona brought forward I had experienced a lifetime on Dakote, which is one of the planets that circle the sun Taygeta in the Pleiades. Interestingly, her and Tolec have also experienced lifetimes on Dakote. It made so much sense to me then why I had such a burning desire to meet them physically!

The Pleiades is also known as the seven sisters.

As with Earth, the experiment of duality has been carried out on many other Planets so there are Service to self beings (negative / dark) and Service to others (positive / light).

Keep in mind this is my understanding / belief regarding this subject so if you don't resonate with what I say please feel free to disregard it.

I have been speaking Light Language for quite a while now and I am fascinated listening to the many other dialects which are being both spoken and sung. My friend, Lightstar in Couldville, speaks many different Light Languages and has videos of them on You Tube.

It is truly wonderful how many Starseeds are taping themselves speaking the Light Language and sharing it on FB as well as in YouTube videos. Many places are being created to support people beginning to speak Light Language such as on the ECETI Ranch that my friend John took a group of newbies and encouraged them to trust and allow the Light Language to come through. James Gilliland runs the ECETI Ranch which is near Mount Adams. There is a lot of UFO activity there.

James runs a lot of Workshops on his Ranch, including doing Night Watches. My experience of speaking Light Language is I never know what is going to come out my mouth. Some people can translate what is spoken. When I first began speaking I had heard others speak it. Suddenly it just began falling out of my mouth, there is no conscious thought of what the next sound is going to be, it just flows, and the Ships respond which is important!

When I see the UFO's / Ships, I speak Light language and they "Power up", becoming brighter and larger, enabling me to video them! Mind you, just because they are relatively close to the horizon does not mean you will get a clearer video! The Golden Triangle I videoed came out on my camera as a blurry grey / blue circle. When I spoke to them more in Light Language, they then showed themselves on my camera as a larger brilliant white circle. I had to try several times to actually get them to show themselves on the video. I was quite surprised because the rectangular Golden Ship that I videoed right above my head, came out much clearer and was very much further away from me!

Pre Couldville

It was only recently I discovered I had received Galactic downloads as a child. I was still in Primary School and for a short while we went horse riding after church. I remember being very excited doing this, getting changed in the back seat of the car. A lady I recently met, who has a powerful Galactic connection, asked me if I had ever done horse riding as a child. It took me a wee while to remember as it hadn't happened for very long. Honestly I was quite intrigued as to why she asked. When she explained to me I had received Galactic Downloads whilst engaged in this activity I was extremely surprised. She works a lot with the Galactics and confirmed that I am Pleiadian. This was the second confirmation I had received. I have since had a third confirmation by a Past Life Reader.

I remember my parents telling me that I was extremely sick and almost died not long after I was born. Dad arranged for a Mass to be said for me and apparently I began recovering after this was done.

My adult version of this is we are Spirit having a human experience, on a Soul level I chose to come to assist with the Ascension of this planet like I had done with many other planets beforehand. This however was going to be far more challenging as this was a very dense third dimensional planet and I was used to working with planets of much higher vibrations. I have had many incarnations here and I probably felt I had enough of this, I just wanted to go home but my Sky Family reminded me of the Contract I had made and promptly sent me back down here!

Keeping this experience in mind, in a way I am not surprised I was receiving Galactic downloads as a child, I had important work to do as do all Starseeds here at this present time. The service to self, negative Aliens here had prevented us from Ascending earlier on and this now is the final push from those of the Light to achieve Ascention this time around! We are holding up the Ascension of, in my understanding, the whole of the Milky Way which is why there are so many Craft in our atmosphere now! My understanding is that on the 17th November 2017 the Plaedians were given permission from much higher up the chain of command, Ashtar Command I believe, to step in and assist humanity achieve Ascension this time around.

I can hear many people asking, "Do you believe in God??", absolutely I believe in Great White Spirit as my Native American brothers and sisters refer to God as. There are many names for the Creator. We won't go into the gods / Annunarki that played with DNA and created quite a variety of different life forms. That is in the too hard, cannot wrap your mind around it subject. I have had people ask me in the past if I am a god fearing woman. I say NO! My God is very loving and kind, not vengeful which are gods (Annunarki) in my understanding. Just thought I would throw that out there. Has anyone else noticed that discrepancy? I have disassociated with religion due to the divisions.

Okay, in for a penny in for a pound as the old saying goes. While we are playing in this very deep "Rabbit hole" of subjects that are rarely discussed, let's talk a bit about Multi-dimensional time lines. There is no Past or Future, there is only the NOW!!!This is something that took me a very long time to wrap my head around so I can imagine it will put many into absolute overwhelm!! All these Past Lives and

Future Lives we are living simultaneously due to multidimensional time lines!!! In my understanding, sometimes there is a "leaking" from one time line to the next so we "remember" other lifetimes!

As a Spiritualist I believe we go through the "Grey mists of Forgetfulness" every time we Reincarnate so we can focus on one lifetime at a time, this one!! WOW!!! There are children being born now who come in with memories of their Past Lives, very advanced Old Souls with knowledge far beyond their years!

When I moved up here in 2004, I began working with a Psychic Group who travelled around various Shopping Centres, staying there for a week at a time. I worked for this group for many years and met some amazing Psychics, some of whom were Starseeds themselves.

Blue has been my favourite colour for years, in fact I got to the point where I firmly believed that at some stage, many lifetimes ago on another Planet, I had actually had blue skin. Well Robert from FB actually confirmed that for me when he connected me to my Andromedian family. He informed me he had never seen anyone with such blue skin as my mother who had come through to do some Energy Healing on me. No wonder the knowing of having blue skin was so strongly imprinted into my memory! This event confirmed to me I was indeed a Starseed and I had come with a very important mission to be a part of. It is awesome when you get these kinds of confirmations. When you just feel within yourself that there is something important you are meant to be doing, you begin to wonder if you are imagining things. Someone else very precious to me came through with my mother during that day, he was my Andromedian partner. Robert told me to step in front of him energetically and asked me if I could see a ring on his left middle finger. I was able to sense it as my Clairvoyant abilities are not very strong as yet. Robert then asked me to look above that ring to see another ring on top of it, I could sense it. Robert then instructed me to put my middle right finger into that ring. Now you might say, you imagined it, but I had my girlfriend in Couldville, who is Clairvoyant to look at my right hand and describe what she saw without telling her what had happened.

She described to me a ring with a violet flame on the top of it. I felt so deeply honoured to receive this ring from my Andromedian partner.

I am very grateful to Robert for doing the work he does and connecting us to our Andromedian families. All who are ready to be connected are drawn to him by our families. You need to be ready for this, in a space of Love!

Connecting with Couldville

I don't remember how I found out about Couldville but it just called to me, I was absolutely fascinated about it! Energetically it felt like I was being called "home" on some level I really didn't understand at that time. I searched in Libraries, Book stores, even Travel Agencies to get more information on this elusive place not many people had even heard of, even the Travel Agencies that focused on flights to America and Tours of America. It was like looking for hens teeth as the saying goes! Ever so gradually I collected more bits of information about it. Remember, there was not much information available on Couldville and I was really blessed to be able to book into the Super 8 Motel in West Couldville. One day I came across a book that actually contained a map of Couldville. It spoke of four major Electro Magnetic Vortices. I had no idea what they were so needed to do more research. I was clueless as to what Energy was back then.

I was a catholic that had been raised in a State School and went to mass every Sunday to hear it in Latin which of course I didn't understand but I learnt all the responses! When I went to High School Latin was offered but that was for the kids who wanted to become doctors and that wasn't me so I learnt French. It came in handy when I went to New Zealand and worked at the Rawhiti Trust Private Hospital in Mount Eden, Auckland. I could see One Tree Hill from outside my room window, the tree was actually still there then. Anyway, a lot of our clients there were rich Tahitians who spoke French! The Tahitians would gift us with shell necklaces when they left the hospital to all those who took care of them. I was the only non-Tahitian who got to go to dinner with them before they went back home, such a beautiful memory. Anyway, back to this map of Couldville and these Electro Magnetic Vortices. Boynton Canyon, Cathedral Rock and Red River Crossing (they are in the same area), Airport Messa and Bell Rock. Well Bell Rock really jumped out at me, I felt so drawn to it and didn't get to understand why till I went back in 2012. What surprised me was that Bell Rock was literally in the shape of a Bell. Does that seem odd to anyone else? When I went back to Couldville in 2012 and I was told Bell was actually a Ship in the form of a rock.

It made sense to me why Bell had been calling me for 30 years beforehand, I believe that an aspect of me was very familiar with that Ship! Apparently some Uni students tried to send it back up into space I was told. People who live in VOC (Valley of Oak Creek), often would see lights coming and going from Bell. To me that made so much sense of why Scout Ships come and go from there. Does anyone else resonate with this energy? Couldville is such an amazing place!

I tried saving my money so I could go but children came along and my dream of going to Couldville was pushed to the back burner. I had to wait until they grew up and that very minor detail of having money to be able to go, manifested once my parents crossed to the other side of Life, Thirty years was a very long wait, felt like 60 years it dragged by so slowly.

Talking about time you do realise it is manmade and so I have found over the years the 'speed' with which it passes varies greatly depending on whether you are really enjoying something (I find it generally goes real fast then) or you are waiting for something really important to happen, then it goes real slowly! I don't know about anyone else but I also find the older I get the faster time seems to go as well. It isn't just me however because I have spoken to my 30 year old daughter who has five children and she finds time seems to have sped up for her as well.

Anyway, I eventually got my parents' inheritance and my partner at the time wanted me to use it to buy a house for us. I have got to admit, I went into severe depression at the very thought of never being able to achieve my dream of going to Couldville.

Don't get me wrong, having your own home is something that is very important to many people but I had been holding onto this deep burning passionate desire to be in Couldville for the last 30 years and I didn't want to give up on my dream, so deep in me!

I used to do Readings in Shopping Centres and this day we were working outside a Travel Agency! That day changed my life!!! Instead of having lunch I went straight to the Travel Agency and booked my Flight and Accommodation! I was victorious! My long held onto dream was going to manifest after long last!

Needless to say my partner wasn't very happy but I was over the Moon! I am sure there are many of you that can relate to making a life changing decision on the spur of the moment. Sometimes we just need to take that leap of faith when we feel something is really calling us, so I held my nose and I jumped!

When I originally made the booking I was coming home at the end of October 2011. It took a couple of days to realise about the 11th November 2011. There was no way I was being home for that major event! My children had grown up with knowing how important 11.11 was for me. My friend just laughed at me and was wondering when I was going to realise the importance of that November so I extended my stay till the 5th December so I could have my Mum's birthday over there as well.

So finally I was able to check out all the electromagnetic vortices in Couldville physically, so much joy I felt finally being able to be there after waiting for so long! Many people find the energy there too powerful so they are unable to stay for very long. I met one guy who was only able to stay a couple of hours the first time he was there! I understand from locals there that many relationships tend to break up there when one of the partners are a higher vibration than the other one. People with low vibrations find the very high vibrations in Couldville very challenging to deal with I am led to understand by locals. The veil is very thin in Couldville so there is a lot of Ships that make themselves visible, even in the form of Cloud Ships! Have you ever seen a cloud with lines on it in an unusual shape? It isn't a cloud! I took many photos of them when I was there in 2012. I even had one in the shape of a bell come outside my room window. As soon as I got the photo of it, it dissipated, blew me away!

I experienced so many first experiences whilst I was in Couldville, it is such a magical place. Things such as dancing in falling snow, being stung by a bee, experiencing snow from Couldville to the Grand Canyon, seeing Cloud Ships and regular UFO's, meeting some amazing people who are still my friends to this day. Lightning struck the power pole right outside the Super 8 and created a fire while it was still raining. My eyes got so badly sunburned while I was doing a floating meditation in the pool, they were puffy for days! I learned to wear sunglasses from then on whilst I was doing the floating meditations.

I had a guy tell me he was from Sirius B, I mean only in Couldville! I was aware of the Galactic Federation of Light before I went but discovered Ashtar Command whilst I was there. Bryan de Flores was running workshops connecting with them. I bought the meditation cd and have played it for years every night. Meeting my beautiful precious SiStar, (a sister from the stars in other words,) Tina, at the Healing workshop Brian ran, was such an memorable experience, like I had known her for so many Lifetimes. I am sure I have! I am so blessed to have her in my life, we have such a deep connection with Ancient Egypt as does my friend Loraine.

I did a mini Vision Quest while I was there to the Birthing Cave with a beautiful couple Jim and Sue Graywolf Petruzzi and their beautiful fur baby Onyx who shared the back seat of their car with me on many journeys. They had only just rescued Crystal from the Pine Ridge Reservation at that stage, she was in a very bad state!

I have balance issues and damaged knees so I don't hike, plus the fact since I had Glandular Fever as a 9 year old my energy level has been very bad so doing this hike to and from the Birthing Cave was absolutely massive for me. I remember as we began an Eagle (Wombli), was flying overhead.

I remember being given a walking stick to assist me. Next thing I know we are nearing the Medicine Wheel and I realise I no longer have the stick which puzzled me greatly. I had never experienced "Missing Time" before. It wasn't until I was on my way back that I found out how great a distance I had been totally unaware of walking.

The path up to the Birthing Cave was very steep and it zigzagged. Jim told me many people were unable to make it to the cave from the Medicine Wheel but I knew I was meant to do it as it was a part of my Vision Quest. Well there were many cacti on that steep rocky path and I managed to connect with one of them! The rocky uneven ground was a bit of a challenge to my balance, or should I say, the weakness in my balance.

Well, I finally made it into the main cave but was unable to enter the Birthing Cave part of it which was right up the back and up a fairly steep sloping wall, for me anyway. A few people managed to enter the "womb" part of the Birthing Cave. Jim lent me his walking stick to assist me back down from the Cave and I had a couple of people assisting me. Someone took off with my camping stool that I used to rest on so I just had to keep walking. I felt so blessed that a beautiful young man, Bill, stayed with me all the way back to the car park. I was so overwhelmed on the way back because I did not recognise the areas we were walking through due to my 'missing time' on the way there. I would have been terribly lost without him, thank you Mr O'Mara.

Once I entered the cave I was amazed at how high up we were! The view was magnificent. The reason the path was zig zag made a lot of sense once I got to the cave! Climbing up to the cave really brought me into being in the present moment big time! I was focusing intently on where I was placing my feet on the pathway and being extremely aware of the closeness of the cacti there. It was a momentary lack of balance that connected me with a cacti on my ascent into the cave. I "got the point" quite literally of how this journey was a mini Vision Quest for me. It was definitely quite challenging as I have Osteo Arthritis so I never did Bush walks as my knees were badly affected. I felt very blessed to have connected with Jim, Sue and Onyx.

I spent a considerable amount of time with them when they were in Couldville. Jim and Bearcloud are friends so I was blessed to be able to do two Inipis with them.

My Journey in Couldville 2011 and 2012

It seemed like a dream come true waiting at Brisbane airport to board the plane for Los Angeles. It was raining when I eventually landed. I didn't sleep much on the plane but watched movies and occasionally realised I had missed a hunk of the movie

I spent many hours getting to Phoenix and then there was the 2 hour bus trip to Couldville. I was very blessed that the Super 8 where I was staying was one of the stops the bus made so that made things easy for me, the energies there are very powerful and I did a lot of sleeping for a few days after I arrived. Of course jet lag played a wee part also. Apparently Couldville is at a very high elevation also I recently was told by my girlfriend who lives there and that was another reason why the first few days I spent out of body! Apparently high elevations make you very sleepy!

It didn't take long before I had my first massive experience. I found myself waking up rubbing my left hip. My first thought of course was "Why am I doing this?? What a bizarre thing to do as you are waking up!" Slowly it dawned on me that my hip was rough and my mind started racing like,

"Why does my hip feel rough?' "What happened to me last night?" I quickly got out of bed to check out my hip. I had to really twist my body around before I eventually saw 3 holes surrounded by serous fluid, which is why it was rough! The holes were evenly spaced like a machine of some kind had created them. They differed in depth, shallow, medium then the last one was the deepest. How did I know they differed in depth? I guess I just sensed it, and perhaps the amount of serous fluid around the holes might have been another indication for me.

The first thing I did was race next door to a young Canadian girl who was staying at the Super 8 for three weeks. Excitedly I called to her whist knocking rapidly on her door, Tammy! Tammy!, look what happened to me last night! Interestingly she had also had a strange experience that night as well. Her brother has passed over and she was aware of him being with her, she is Clairvoyant! Witness number one and yes, 7 years later I still have contact with her on FB.

I had done a Give Away with a beautiful English couple a couple of nights before so they were the next people I showed my hip to so I have 3 witnesses to this experience.

It took me a couple of days to realise there was absolutely no pain! I would never have known about that experience if I hadn't woken up rubbing my hip. I have a very low pain threshold so it isn't like I have a high pain threshold and I blocked out the pain! It took me another few days, I was in a wee bit of shock after all, before I began to question why the serous fluid had actually coagulated around the holes. A couple of things I took into consideration, I was lying on my side, we have a thing called Gravity down here so why hadn't the serous fluid just run down my hip? When you injure yourself the serous fluid doesn't instantly coagulate, it takes quite a while!

This led me to believe that I felt that where this occurred there was no gravity and I was there for a considerable amount of time in order for the coagulation to take place. Sky Family is very good at manipulating time!

In my understanding the veil in Couldville is very thin so there is a lot of UFO activity there. Now I was very familiar with the Galactic Federation of Light before I went over to Couldville so the way my mind processed this experience was that I must have been taken up onto the UFO for this to have taken place. I understand ET's vibrate at a much higher vibration than we do down here in 3D, so they can walk through 3D walls because of their higher vibration. My belief is that as I am a Starseed and have experienced lifetimes not only here but on many other Planets. I believe that the ET's are able to shift my energies so they are able to take my physical body through 3D walls / windows etc and up to the Craft. I also believe ET's don't do time like us but they can manipulate time / space when they travel vast distances so when they take us onto the Craft maybe it is in 3D time, maybe it isn't.

This was my very first experience in waking up with things that I didn't go to sleep with. I often I wake up with scratch marks which I photograph and share with my friends. One morning I woke up with a couple of red marks near my left elbow, one looked like a rectangle. The next day they began to blister! Once again, there was no pain, Over the next week those blisters got quite big and one even got infected so I went to the doctor and he took a swab and sent off to identify what had caused the infection.

When he got the result back the Lab had not been able to identify what had caused the infection!

What a surprise! I was told it was due to an allergic reaction to the implant they placed there. This makes a massive amount of sense as to why they couldn't identify the source of the infection.

Those blisters got quite huge and I showed several friends so yeah, I have witnesses for that experience as well, not to mention the doctor and my friend, his receptionist! These are the two biggest things that I have woken up with, There have been several interesting bruises and scratch marks.

One of the scratch marks I received was on my abdomen, they looked like grazes they were quite wide. I was actually in hospital when that happened so I had nurses as witnesses to that experience!

Needless to say that freaked them out severely as you are under constant monitoring! They couldn't wrap their heads around how that had happened and the size of the grazes being so large! They were just a tad obvious for the nurses who assisted showering me. I have never experienced grazes like that before. Normally they are scratches, often looking like they have dots along them. Often these dots don't appear for a couple of days so in my understanding, these dots make the scratches different from a normal scratch.

I just did a Night Watch last night and woke up with a very long straight scratch mark with a bruise beside it and a smaller scratch mark towards the outside of my leg at a different angle. There is no pain with these particular scratches. The long scratch mark is easy to see on the top part of my left leg near to my knee. Most of my scratch marks have not been as easy to find like under my breast or on the side of my abdomen. It is like who ever does these marks were like trying to hide them so I wouldn't find them. Now they make them more obvious. Sometimes, very rarely I have found them after water gets on them and they sting but that rarely happens. I feel they are very fresh when this happens. I will say that the lack of pain and the unusual places, like under my breast, makes them challenging for me to be aware of them.

I have photographed these scratches and blisters and have shown many of my friends so I have lots of witnesses!

In 2011 Melinda was just starting her business of doing UFO Night Tours in Couldville. She used Army Night vision goggles to assist you to see the Ships clearer. Cathedral Rock is the place where they "blink out". If they pass over Cathedral Rock they are satellites!

That was the first time I had ever seen UFO's, they were bright extremely fast moving objects, very high up. It was fascinating for me to see the difference between the UFO's and the Satellites. There is no way you can confuse Satellites with the very fast erratically moving Craft. We were blessed with quite a clear sky which really helps. So annoying when clouds obscure the view!

In 2012 I discovered Cloud Ships! A Bell shaped Ship parked itself outside my window until I got a photo of it then it disappeared! I found that fascinating! It was like they were calling to me so I would notice them, and once I took the photo they were satisfied. That is what it felt like to me anyway! I took the photos on a phone camera I had bought from the Circle K across the road from the Super 8.

The road outside the Super 8 is known as 89A and is a very busy road. Back then there were no traffic lights to help you across, I understand there are some there now. On the way back from uptown Couldville on the bus one day, there was a lady on the bus who described the method she used to cross the road. I was fascinated, on the way to her stop she just visualised the road was clear, and sure enough, when she got off, it was, so I tried it and it worked for me as well! I was very grateful to her!

The Managers son was working there when I went back in 2012. Now Greg is very much into the UFO's. One day he suggested I go out the back to see the Rod Ships. These ones were not Cloud Ships but look like a cylinders just hanging there.

My most amazing experience happened when I was on the way back to the Lobby!

Parked over the Super 8 car park was a Cloud Ship parked on its side. There was a small black cloud exposed and I knew that was the entrance!

Well there I was in a foreign country, my passport was upstairs and I just had to let Greg know I was going for a wee ride! I recalled how people were sometimes returned miles away from where they were picked up so that is why I wanted to let him know what I was planning on doing, When I went up the back to check out the Rod Ships the car park was clear of cars, and there was no Cloud Ship in sight! I believe after they had put the tracking device in my hip, my belief was that they had come deliberately to pick me up! If I could have that time again I would walk straight into that Ship!

When I came back out with Greg in tow it was nowhere in sight! I was so disappointed! Even now, six years later I still regret not walking into that cloud ship! The way I see it was maybe Greg was not meant to see it. They deliberately came I believe, for me!!! What a massive honour that was and I screwed it up. I so wish I could turn time back. I wasn't scared, I just wanted someone to know that I was going for a wee trip because I wasn't sure how long I would be gone.

The next day one of the staff who lived in Cottonwood was telling everyone about this massive Cloud Ship larger than a football oval people had witnessed. The first thing I thought was, "That was the Ship that came to pick me up!" I felt a bit better that there were others that had witnessed it as well.

About a week later you could have knocked me over with a feather when I saw a picture of it on FB floating just above the house roofs. I have photos on my American Phone, minor detail, I have moved and have no idea where the camera or charger for it is. I will have to ask my Sky family to help me find it. Sadly my phone was up in my room when the Ship decided to land on the car park so I never got to take a photo of it to show other people, but I will never forget that experience!

Only in Couldville, the veil is so thin and the vibrations there are quite high and the Spiritual Community there is very aware of them. My experience of Couldville was that there are two different communities there. The Spiritual Community and the Art Community

The Art Community often seem to be unaware of the Spiritual Community. Bearcloud is a local artist, who runs his own Art Gallery in the valley of Oak Creek, is very aware of UFO activity. He goes to England to check out the Crop Circles and has spoken at the Star Knowledge Conferences.

Chief Golden Light Eagle actually retains the memory of being on the Ships and receiving information from his Star Family. He was told to share the information he receives which is why he runs the Star Knowledge Conferences.

I often visited the Centre of New Age in Couldville. I had my Aura Photograph taken and she explained the colours and gave me a Reading on it. People do Healing Modalities, run Tours and do Readings from there. They also have a range of Crystals and many other fascinating things to check out.

I had gone to Re-Member at Pine Ridge Reservation to do a week's volunteer work for the Olgala Sioux for a week in October, 2011. We were the last group to be there for the year. This was something I arranged to do before I left Australia due to my Past Life connection with the Sioux and the fact they are one of the poorest Reservations in America at that time.

I was bitten several times by a large black spider which was eventually found when they washed all my clothes, it was hiding in my suitcase. Anyway my right ankle became very painful afterwards. Walking became extremely challenging so I bought a camp stool when I got back home to Couldville. One of the Healers I met was Stands With Bear (SWB). He says his father is Ashtar from Ashtar Command. He is a truly amazing Hollow Bone and did an amazing Healing session with me. It was challenging trying to walk afterwards because his Healing had been so powerful!! Crossing the road to catch the bus was an extremely interesting / challenging, exercise!

When I got back to the Golden Goose they were very concerned for me because I was so "Out of it!" My ankle began improving from there on. It took a long time till I was totally pain free however. I still have that stool, my lifesaver!

Another very interesting person I met at the Centre of New Age was Melinda Leslie. She was just beginning her UFO Night Watch Tours, only in Couldville! She was having issues getting the Night Vision Goggles for her clients to see the Ships (UFO's) clearer. She came to me for a Reading regarding the success of her business as she was questioning herself as to whether she was meant to do it.

I informed her that her business would grow and thrive and I was correct. It has taken off so well she does Day Tours as well as the Night Tours. She speaks on radio shows, presents at Conferences, she has really taken off! Cathedral Rock is a portal for the UFO's. You can tell the difference between the UFO's and Satellites because the UFO's blink out over Cathedral Rock, Satelites keep going!

If you ever find yourselves in Couldville, I strongly suggest you do a UFO Sky Watch with Melinda Lesley! She is on FB and over the years she has posted many videos of Craft. Couldville is an absolute hot spot for UFO activity! I would love to personally thank Melinda for holding onto her dream and following through with it as she has now shared these Tours with thousands of people since 2012.

When I went back to Couldville in 2012 it was July, August and Thunder storm season! The UFO's disguise themselves as clouds with lines on them! My girlfriend in Couldville sent me a photo of Bell Rock and right beside it was a very unusual cloud looking like one of those collapsing plastic bowls with the lines down the bottom of it! I saw a cloud that looked like a bell, it came in front of my room window at the Super 8 and as soon as I got the photo of it, it dissipated!

I was so thrilled when I learnt about the Cloud Ships! What a perfect disguise for people who are not AWAKE and AWARE, all they see is clouds and they don't even question the unusual shapes so our Sky Family can come in real close to us without severely freaking people out and causing mass panic! Those of us Starseeds who are awake and aware gain much delight in knowing our Sky Family is so close to us!! I really enjoyed watching the sky and searching for the Cloud Ships.

How Couldville has changed my life

This experience made me realise that I was indeed a Starseed! That is the only conclusion I could come to as to why I wake up with scratch marks, why I experienced those puncture marks when I first arrived there and why a Cloud Ship would land in the Super 8 car park to pick me up! There was nobody else around except for Greg who was working in the Lobby. I KNEW I was seeing a massive Cloud on the ground that retained a circular shape. By any stretch of the imagination, this was NOT NORMAL! It was on its side, since when does a normal cloud do things like that? The entrance was a black cloud, the rest of the cloud was white, there was a distinct colour difference! I often wonder what would have happened if I had walked into it, regretfully I will never know. I could tell it was like a convex and concave shape with windows around the middle of it, don't ask me how I knew there were windows around the middle, I just felt it! A week later someone had put a photo of the Cloud Ship floating just above the roof tops on FB! My heart sang with joy, to see a photo of the Cloud Ship that had landed in the Super 8 car park to pick me up! Confirmation for me that I had not imagined it. I do wish I had thought of taking a photo of the photo of it on FB! I just never thought of doing that at the time! Much later I saw a photo of the physical Ship and instantly recognised it as the Ship that had come for me and yes, there was a row of windows between the two plates which I had felt there was!

RESOURCES for Healing Inner Childhood wounds for Starseeds!

My long-time friend in Couldville Tina Campbell does Inner Child work as well as many other modalities.

Her email address is 2u.loveandlight@gmail.

Please feel free to email her for further information and prices.

Tina will do Skype sessions with you so you don't have to be physically in Couldville to work with her.

This was definitely the trigger that got me interested in doing Night Watches. My friend Robyn took me to my first one down on the Gold Coast, the lady who runs it had been working with the Greys for many years. Robyn had had some very negative experiences with the Greys so she freaked out rather severely when she found out that the lady running the Night Watch worked with the Greys.

I was able to say to her, not all Greys are negative, these Greys are in the energy of Service to others, not service to self. Many ET's who have Light Bodies will use the body of a Grey in order to deal with the lower vibration, dense energy of 3D, so just because they look like a Grey does not mean they are Greys! It is the most suitable overcoat for these beings to use!

I had a photo taken at that Night Watch which showed a blue Orb over my head. That was more confirmation to me that I was different to many people. That was the second time I had seen the picture of an Orb. The one I saw in Couldville contained geometric shapes, I was fascinated!

It took me a while to connect with a Night Watch on the north side here. Jason ran this group. I went a few times and then he stopped doing them. I did make several new friends from these Night Watches. One of my friends Bernie had just done a Dolores Cannon hypnotherapy session and I told him he was Reptilian, which he confirmed. He was taken onto the Ship during his session and was shown his Reptilian body. This was actually a massive learning curve for me because up till then I had tarred all Reptilians with the same brush, that they were all low vibrational. We need to remember we live in an existence of Duality, and this isn't just restricted to the Earth Plane.

I attended UFO Meetings at Mango Hill with Kristy. I went one night to a new venue in Deagon, it was the first time I had been there and I had been driving for around 35 minutes and pulled up to identify clearer where the hall was. It was raining, after I identified I could park closer I went back to the car to bring it closer to the hall. Can you imagine my surprise when I tried to turn the car on and nothing worked.

Believe me I was really puzzled but figured I would get the RACQ out after the meeting, We had a Medium giving us Readings that night. I had an ET come through for my message, then the penny dropped. I had heard of many cases where people's cars had just stopped working when there was a UFO around so I went back to my car and sure enough she started without any problem! They just wanted to make sure I got their message for me!

How many of you have ever had a similar experience? I must admit I was quite confused by it at first seeing I had just been driving the car. I had listened to my intuition to attend the meeting, it all fell into place once I received my message. I understand my Sky Family has been with me since I was born and my many Past Lives as well. I feel so safe and protected with them at all times!. Can any of you relate to how I feel?

As on Earth ET's have many Races and each of these Races have many different dialects. We refer to the Language they speak as Light Language. It is a Soul to Soul communication which the logical mind cannot interpret so many people find it challenging to listen to because they want to understand what is being said through their logical minds. I speak it and know of many others that speak it also. When I first began speaking Light language my Sky Family connected me with a group who did Light Language meditations. This first group I attended held monthly meetings in the local library of a weekend when it was closed to the public.

I had done a 6 day Energy Retreat with Brita. One of the exercises Brita gave us was to speak Light Language. Brita did house sits while she was in Australia, one of the places was not far from where I live. It was one of the members of our group that had gone on holidays, so I was able to spend more time with her physically. I had been doing the meditations for a while by then so was very comfortable in speaking Light Language but several members of our group found it an extremely challenging task to do.

I found it very interesting to look back and see how my Sky Family connected me with a lady who in turn spoke Light Language and introduced me into the meditation Group. When it is time for you to start speaking Light Language our Sky Family creates these links very subtly. I found I had other things in common with the lady they chose to connect me with so they created a solid foundation between us before she mentioned Light Language, I am chuckling to myself how smoothly it happened.

Many are now posting videos of themselves in private rooms speaking Light Language, such a wide variety of languages as well as dialects of the same Group of ET's. John runs one such room which I am a member of. He has spent time on the ECETI Ranch with James whom I met in person when he came out to Australia. I was in Tramville at the time so connected with Peter. We did an amazing Sky Watch on the beach and one of the Ships "powered up" very brightly, many times the original size of it then disappeared! Funny enough I had seen only a couple of days before hand, a video of a Ship "Powering up" and I decided I really wanted to see one of those in real life. My wish was granted and I feel so blessed. I have seen others "power up" since but not near as big as that particular Ship!

I just love the way the web of connection expands, one of your friends knows someone you don't then you are connected. I just love connecting with other Starseeds here on Earth as we are scattered far and wide and often feel very lonely because we are often the :black sheep" of our family. They simply do not understand us and we feel even more like outsiders! Many of us look up at the skies and long to go "Home" but we have no idea where that is. The interesting thing is we do not come from just one planet, we have incarnated on many. Most Humanoids originated on Lyra but because it was attacked by the Reptilians, we had to flee before they destroyed our planet so we were scattered far and wide across the Galaxies!

Compared to Human life span, the life spans of ET's can be hundreds, if not thousands of years so a mere 100 years here is like a blink of an eye to them. Even though to us here it feels like an extremely long time!

Those of us who volunteered to come here have assisted many other Planets to Ascend, Mother Earth is the last one which needs to Ascend then there will be the opportunity for us to become Galactic Cosmic Citizens. There will be two Earths eventually, a 3rd Dimensional one and a 5th Dimensional one. Negative emotions cannot come into 5th Dimension as everything manifests instantaneously there, so LOVE is the only vibration that will allow you to enter it. We have a choice to make, are we ready to release our negative emotions and just focus on the LOVE Vibration?

I eventually connected with Lauren who I now do my Night Watches with. She has had contact with ET'S since she was very young and remembers it clearly! Lauren is very sensitive to their energy and they Telepathically communicate with her as they do with many Empathic Starseeds.

It is like they call us Telepathically to come outside, they then show themselves to us. Damien actually videos the UFO's that call him. I have taken some photos of interesting bright lights in the skies. One is bright green, another is bright white then later on they began flashing red and green as well.

John Bertoli told me that is how Sky Family speak Light Language to us with the flashing green and red lights. These lights are stationary when I see them. Because I only have my phone camera they show up as little white dots. When I expand them they show up with the different colours.

We not only have activity in the sky but also on the ground with Yeti's. Man they make a lot of noise hitting the trees. There was a Clairvoyant lady attending the Night Watch when the Yeti came in, she said it was a youngster. My understanding of Yeti is that they are inter dimensional. The sound kept coming from different directions with 20 minute or so pauses in between so it wasn't constant. I could sense him jumping in and out of the 3rd Dimension.

Lauren has had a long connection with ET and the Ships. This is why I enjoy doing her Night Watches. We do it up a mountain with very few houses around. She trained with Steven so uses his tapes, toning and bowls to raise the vibration. ET will only contact us and show themselves when everyone has an open Heart, sending Love to them They will never interact with anyone who is holding fear of them so this is something Lauren strictly scrutinises who comes to the Group. She has Protocols in place, everyone must do the session on Protocols before they are permitted to do the Night Watch.

I just love the way Lauren uses the Native American tradition of smudging with White Sage as we begin Circle, and yes, we do sit in a circle, brilliant for clearing unwanted Energies. She also uses Crystals and we place our own crystals in the centre of the circle with hers. Interestingly, when it is cold there is often more activity in the skies. Often when there is a lot of cloud around we all send the request to the ET's to clear the sky for us which they lovingly do so we can see them. We are so blessed to have such a brilliant connection with them. On one occasion the ET's were walking around the circle giving us Healing Energy, it was such an awesome, amazing experience!

Once I came home I began waking up with scratch marks that were not there when I went to bed. I even experienced red patches which turned into blisters and became quite large. There is absolutely NO PAIN when these things happen. If they are very fresh they will sting when I get into the shower, otherwise I would be ignorant of them being there unless I notice them in the mirror or when I am showering. Recently I am getting these scratch marks while I am awake, talking on the phone, answering my emails, doing my FB. Oh man, they really stung, out of the blue.

Simon speaks of the Black Ops Military abducting people who have already been abducted by the Greys mostly and they are being scratched by a tac or a nail. News for you Simon, some of us are having these experiences when we are wide awake without being abducted.

They just pop into 3rd Dimension from the 4th or 5th. I was sitting at my desk thinking, "Why is my leg suddenly stinging? I haven't moved it and there is nothing sharp under my table. I would love to be able to add some of my photos but they were just taken on my phone so I don't know if the quality is good enough to be able to do it.

I take photos of these marks so I can share the evidence with others who are heavily involved in the UFO Community such as Mary and Damien. I share them with Lauren and others involved with the UFO Research Community. I have plenty of witnesses.

There is no pain unless they are extremely freshly done. I just discover them when I am having a shower or checking in the mirror. I found them in very unusual places at first but now they are often in obvious places.

One morning I woke with 2 red marks near my left elbow. The next day small blisters appeared which continued to get larger over the next week. Once again, there was no pain! One of the large blisters became infected so I went to the doctor so the cause of the infection could be identified. When I went back for the results the lab had been unable to identify the cause of the infection so he couldn't prescribe antibiotics for me I was told that I had experienced an allergic reaction to the implant they had put there, hence the infection. No wonder the Labs couldn't identify the organism creating the infection. Gunter got to see the blisters at their biggest and also my friend who is the receptionist at the doctors so there were 2 witnesses to this. Of course I took photos as well and shared them with others in the UFO Community. I was shocked how massive the blisters became. Gradually over time they reduced in size and disappeared, the red areas stayed pink and remained quite visible for about a month, like new scar tissue. The only other time I had a very unusual experience is when I woke up one morning rubbing my hip, it was rough which startled me considerably as it made absolutely no sense to me as to why this would be so! I jumped out of bed and went straight to the large mirror. I could see the very side of my hip, there I found 3 puncture wounds., serous fluid had coagulated around the holes which is why it was rough. I had only been in Couldville for about a week.

Other experiences with ET Beings There is a British ex Minister who publicly came out before he was elected and shared his story of being aware of having a Mantid Being as his mother and his father was a Reptilian. He kept telling his human mother she wasn't his mother when he was young as he had a lot of contact with his Alien parents. He made many you tube videos of his journey. Simon Parkes is his name and you can check out several videos he has on you tube.

According to Simon, Mantid Beings are Telepathic. This Telepathy is the way most of the ET's communicate with us I understand. They are the doctors and surgeons. According to a couple of Mantid Hybrids, the Mantids created the Greys. Their names are Robert and Jaqueline and the video is called, Meet the Hybrids, a conversation about the Mantis Beings.

Now there are many different types of Greys. The small 3 foot one tends to be a "worker" Grey. These are involved in the Abductions. They are the ones responsible when Abductees come back with their clothes on back to front for example. Simon says the Mantid Beings get quite frustrated with these ones for pulling stunts like this. According to Simon, the Reptilians, Greys and Mantid Beings are often on the one Ship.

Now I have had my own experiences with a Mantid Being. In 2015, I eventually had Spinal Surgery after a four year wait. To control the pain that was shooting down my right arm from my shoulder to my elbow, I was prescribed Tramadol and Durotram. Interesting that the damage was actually on the left hand side but what can I tell you, I am creative! Many years later I see posts on FB saying that many people have died from using Tramadol, guess I was being well looked after, I have too much work to do, I am not allowed to exit stage left for many years as yet! The doctor had to ring up to get permission for me to have the Durotram. Mind you I was very tired being on these two medications.

Once again, Brita was on the scene, she gave me a Reading and said she saw a very unusual insect like Mantid Being with me. This Being gave the name of En jah. I discovered later this means "Doctor". As I mentioned before, they have a "hive" mind, like bees, so there is no individuality with them except for their bodies, I may be wrong but this is my present understanding. I have an open mind and am always willing to learn more information.

This particular Mantid Being played a very important role in my Surgery. He operated on my spine in my Astral Body, then guided the Surgeons hands when the actual physical operation was being done!.

As I have said, Brita was the person that gave me this information, I just had a deep "knowing" that what she was telling me was absolutely true. If you are being operated on, you are better off having a Mantid Being rather than a Grey.

I asked Brita if I actually needed to have the physical operation, my mother who is on the other side of life said YES! I had chosen to learn how to "receive" through going through this.

What Mum was talking about is the fact I am a Rescuer, we only know how to give, we suck at receiving! I thought at that stage I had been getting better at that but oh man, I was about to learn it on a much deeper level!

I got a blood clot on my 6th Cervical vertebrae which shut down my left side! I thought I had experienced a stroke! It took me a week to lift up my left leg and 3 months before I could lift my arm above my head. My left hand is still weak so I am still doing the lesson of receiving by having Blue Care take me shopping for heavy things like my Pureau 10 litre water (I don't like Fluoride Sulphate, it is on the Poisons List) and to vacuum and mop my floors, I get tired very quickly!

CHAPTER FOURTEEN

Recent events

I am now facing a double full knee replacement, thanks to my Osteo Arthritis again. A year after my left knee replacement my right knee is still pain free! It just was not happy about having to carry the left knee for all those years! Now the left knee has been replaced, my right knee is much happier

I have asked En Jah to support me with these operations as well. They did Psychic Surgery on my knee last time I saw my Energy Healer. I have the up most confidence that my Sky Family will continue looking after me. In my world I believe we create situations for our own Personal Growth. I understand that I needed to learn how to Receive on a deeper level with my Cervical Surgery, hopefully I have learnt that sufficiently as not to repeat that experience again. Well I have begun experiencing numbness on my outer left leg above my knee on my thigh. My left palm and fingers either tingle or go numb when I lay on my left hand side. Now that is a real issue when you sleep on your side like I do! The doctor has put me on anti-inflammatory medication which has stopped the numbing and the tingling thankfully. My doctor sent a referral to the Royal where I had my previous spinal operation done!

Interestingly I was inspired to ring the hospital to ask if they had received the referral after receiving a call regarding an appointment to have my right knee replaced. It really pays to pay attention to your

Intuition / Gut feeling because I rang Ortho Outpatients Clinic and they had not received my referral so they put me through to Central Referrals and it hadn't been received there either so I am going to my doctor to pick up the referral myself and take it into the hospital. I will take the recent x-rays and CT Scan with me so the Royal can add them to my file!

I would like to be able to release the Arthritis from my body through raising my vibrations higher through speaking more Light Language. There are a lot of videos on You Tube sharing about Light Language. I understand once I raise my vibrations to the level of my Energy Signature, my body will be totally healthy. That is definitely my next goal! I really do not want to be stuck using big Pharma medication for the remainder of my life! I like doing things alternatively, if you haven't already realised this with the Energy Healing work I have done! I began using manipulated Molecules called ASEA which gave me excellent pain relief, far better than the Morphine I was on.

Seven weeks after my left total knee replacement I did a Firewalk! I wasn't sure if I could walk that far without my walking frame as my right knee had been playing up as well and my Orthopaedic Specialist has put me on the list for it to be replaced as well. I have a major fear of fire as I had been burnt at the stake as a Witch in Past life. The facilitator looked at me and said I had experienced that on several occasions! I figured that gave me extra reasons for having a fear of fire! The facilitator asked me to come to take part in the Healing aspect of the journey and assured me I didn't have to do the walk.

At one stage in the afternoon he had us go around to each of the other participants and give them a hug! Well, I left my walker by the wall as I didn't want anyone tripping over the extended wheels as I had done when I first got it. I was surprised that I felt quite safe walking around the room without it so I mentioned to the facilitator that I thought I would be able to do the Firewalk. He looked at me with a cheeky smile, his eyes twinkling with delight and informed me that he knew I was going to do the Firewalk when he originally told me about it! It totally blew me away just how powerful the mind truly is! The last step in preparing us for the Firewalk was to take us on a Meditation where we "became" fire! Fire doesn't burn fire! As we walked up to him standing on the edge of the bed of hot coals he would ask us, "Who are you?" Our response was to be, "I am fire!" I was saying this all the time I was walking across the coals. I was unaware of any heat beneath my feet, it was a total surreal experience, like I was dreaming I was doing it.

We stamped our feet when we got to the other end to make sure there were no coals stuck between our toes. He told us to wait till morning before we looked at our feet and to trust our own bodies healing process. He reminded us that if we believed we would have blisters after doing the walk, the brain would dutifully provide them for us! I am pleased to report I experienced just a tingling sensation and I resisted checking the soles of my feet out till the next morning. I had a girlfriend stay with me that night who had also done the walk and I got her to take photos of my feet. The left one where I had the knee replacement was very black indeed, the right one had hardly any black at all. I was buzzing so severely for four days afterwards, such a surreal high at the memory of actually walking on the hot coals without burning my feet. Blows my mind just how powerful the mind truly is!

One of the preparation exercises was walking into an arrow with the blunted point in the soft part of your throat, and snapping it without experiencing any pain in your throat. I had done that exercise many years ago so I knew I was capable of doing it, never questioned it this time around!

Starseed Partners

I have found that many of us Starseeds have come this time to tie up loose ends regarding the relationships we have had from Past Lives, tidying up any karma, so we can then connect with the people who have also been working on themselves so we can complete what we came here to do, together like a team. This has been my experience anyway.

When I met Gunter I remember thinking, this is the man I am going to spend the rest of my life with, yes, we have had many lessons we have chosen to learn together. We have both grown a lot since we first met and played several roles with each other. I began as a boarder with him, man that was a massive learning curve! I got to the point I could no longer live with him, I needed to have my own space. It is interesting, I have tried running away from him so many times but became aware of a very deep Soul Connection between us and realised we have done many, many lifetimes together.

I would take my energetic hook out of him and try to disappear but he always went "fishing" energetically and always managed to reconnect with me. The role I seem to play with him is a "sounding board", he will talk to me about stuff so he can get it straight in his head. I believe it is the role I have chosen to play with him. He keeps me up till 1 or 2am so all aspects of him can have their say. Yeah, that was an interesting journey in itself, getting to know all aspects of him as he is a heavy drinker. I had a Past Life Reading today in an attempt to work out why I feel so deeply connected to Gunter like I have known him for a few thousand years if not Millions. I had a deep feeling he was also a Starseed and yes, today it was confirmed, he is also a Pleiadian! Today I discovered we have chosen to come together to heal the fractured energy between us. It made so much sense to me! It all fell into place!

Neither of my parents drank so dealing with alcoholics and people who drank heavily, was very challenging for me so I need to remind myself, on a Soul Level, I chose to have this experience! When I was told recently that we have an Ancient Soul Contract with each other it resonated so deeply for me and it made sense of why he was able to draw me back in so easily. I had felt that I knew him on such a deep level, finding this out really confirmed what I was sensing with him.

He is such a beautiful friend and I am so grateful to have him in my life, just could never live with him full time again as I work from home now so I very much need my own space. He likes his TV and his music on high volume. It is lovely to sit out the back veranda and watch the storms together when I visit him.

He has been renovating his home for the past 4 years, I have spent thousands of hours talking to him about redesigning his home. My energies saturate that place. He even took many of the inside walls out to redesign the house but he is so afraid of making a mistake he would always keep an open mind just in case he came up with a better idea. He finally put new walls up then deciding the design of the kitchen and bathroom are massive projects which have been the subject of thousands of hours of conversations over the years. I am pleased to announce the kitchen design has now had its final decision and cabinets have been bought and are slowly being put together. Last weekend I went over there and helped him to level the kitchen cabinets so they can now be screwed off to the wall and the bench tops can be joined onto them.

He couldn't see the bubble in the leveller so I played a very important role in doing that. He mentioned to me that he felt we work together very well and I totally agree!

I played a part in choosing the tiles and to see them eventually on the floor was absolutely huge as they had been sitting in stacks for over a year! When he bought them home he didn't realise they had given him some different tiles as well as the ones he wanted. Thank goodness I discovered the discrepancy before he unloaded them from the truck!

A beautiful Chinese concreter was driving past and saw there was a possibility of him getting some extra cash in hand work. He had hit a gold mine, Gunter has many concreting and tiling jobs for him to do! Gunter had been sending out to Spirit for a cash in hand tradesmen to assist him with the house and he was successful in obtaining them! He is a truly brilliant manifestor! I am so proud of him! Gunter even added another carport for any visitors, especially for me, He is still deciding on the design of the bathroom but he will eventually get there.

The last time I stepped back from him I truly realised how much of my energy was in that house of his and how much I really enjoyed contributing my ideas and just being a listening post for him. I was able to go with him to his favourite "Toy Store" to choose plants for the front and back yards. He just adores his hardware stores!

The Bowen Mango tree has recently developed the beginnings of limbs. It really likes it where it has been planted. It now has another batch of red leaves which are the new growth and the branches are growing well. He was so excited when he saw the branches growing, it is now beginning to look like a tree instead of a stick with leaves, I have walked away from Gunter many times but there was always this very deep sense of connection with him. I would take the hook out of me and he would, very shortly after catch me, like a fish, on his fishing line hook and reel me back in again. He didn't get me being a Starseed.

All I wanted was a Starseed partner who understood me, he thought I was a bit weird talking about the UFO's and that I came from another Planet. Poor guy just couldn't wrap his head around it! The interesting thing is today I realised I do have a Starseed friend / partner, he just hasn't realised he is a Pleadian like myself as yet. Slowly he will become aware in his own time. I just need to keep being a Living Example to him. I know in Divine Timing, the penny will eventually drop.

One night, after I had known him for about 6 years, he was really pissed and told me he had been shown the round burn mark that had been left behind by a UFO according to the people he was visiting with his family. Man he had buried that one real deep! When he told me that it gave me a sense of hope. He had recognised that a UFO had been responsible for the circular black mark left behind by using his intuition.

He had said to me if it didn't affect him doing his job or renovating his home, he didn't want to know about it, so he wasn't actually denying the reality of them. Well I had a massive breakthrough in understanding why I felt such a deep connection to him just a month or so ago.

A friend of mine knew a Maori Starseed who connected me to a Starseed in the States

This Maori Starseed suggested I asked the other Starseed to download my Galactic Codes from my Higher Self, that felt real good I must tell you once that was done, I felt deeply Blessed to have made these connections. Anyway the Starseed in the States works with Arch Angel Michael. I happened to mention to him one day about the deep connection I felt with my long term friend and he informed me that was because there was an Ancient Contract between us that had been going on for many, many Lifetimes. Well, when he told me that it made so much sense to me why I felt such a deep connection to him even though I kept running away from him.

Man it feels like a Twin Flame Connection and I am the Runner, big time! I am not saying we are Twin Flames but man, the pattern is surely present!

Anyway Arch Angel Michael was connected for assistance and he dissolved the Ancient Contract between us. All I wanted to do was cry from joy, happiness and relief. The picture I felt was my friend had been encased in this massively thick Ancient cacoon like structure. Once the contract was dissolved, then he was able to be freed from his cacoon. He emerged like this beautiful Golden Being. It was such a beautiful sight to behold. I believe he is also a Starseed, he just needs to Wake Up!

This Ceremony has had physical consequences. He is reducing the amount he smokes and drinks and has even got his appetite back. He hasn't been hungry for years, you can stick him through the eye of a needle however. He even got the courage to remove a tooth which had often had abscesses under it, It was an anchor tooth for his bottom denture and he was concerned it would be too loose. He has a bad gagging reflex.

He got the tiles on the floor and bought the kitchen cupboards and put quite a few together already. Now he just has this wee snag of needing to complete the plastering and painting in the kitchen before he can put the cupboards up. Deciding on the bench tops was a massive decision but he ran his decision past me, I checked them out online and gave him my tick of approval. Now they are delivered!

He has been living in a building site for the past 4 years. He is terrified of making a mistake so hesitates to make a decision just in case a better idea comes along. A massive case of OCD big time! It took me a long time to recognise it in him! Yes, I am his "Sounding Board" that he runs all his ideas past to get things clear in his head.

Just to make life even more interesting for him, he has six different personalities. Depending on how drunk he is, and I have had to form a relationship with each one of them. This was so challenging at first because they thought I was his last girlfriend who had died from Cancer. It took them a while to get my name right.

I have now connected him with the person that took his virginity at 17 so I am now free to connect with my new partner and he is having a wonderful time, no longer trying to hook me back in because he is lonely. After the first couple of months be began calling me again as she would break up with him every time she got drunk. She had a male friend she would help out but was very jealous of my connection with Gunter. I had to remind her I was the person that brought her back into his life!

When she was drunk she would message me on FB for hours telling Gunter she rarely spoke to me. She wanted to be friends and come and meet me which I was fine with. However, I didn't know that she was drunk when she was saying this. I told Gunter and he was not happy about her and I being friends, he didn't have to worry because as soon as she was sober she was no longer interested in connecting with me.

Every time she broke off Gunter would find out that she had blocked him on her phone and Messenger.

Eventually she would unblock him and they would get back together again for a wee while. After a while Gunter had enough of the breaking up with him so the relationship only lasted six months but the good thing that came out of it was that his 21 year old self that asked her to marry him got to find out what it was like to be in an adult relationship with her.

Apparently she stayed with his elder brother and when they split up he had to sell the house. Gunter was very wary of her doing the same thing to him.

Interestingly now the shoe is on the other foot, I have a beautiful man in my life, Gunter refused to talk to me for the first couple of months. My beautiful Twin Flame lives an hour away from me. We go to Meditations, Church and UFO Meetings together.

Now Gunter is understanding why I could never have a relationship with him when he sees all the things my Twin Flame and I do together. All he was interested in doing was drinking and smoking.

I wonder

Through Social Media I have been able to connect with many other Starseeds and Soul Family. Not the intention they had when they created the site, they just wanted to gather our information! Not that you ever put any correct information on your page regarding personal information. I never post personal information on there for that very reason. My job is to plant seeds of information, drip feeding people with tit bits of TRUTH to fulfil my purpose of making people aware of what is really happening behind the scenes, deep down that rabbit hole David Icke speaks of.! So many logical people who are totally out of contact with their intuition who just swallow the rubbish the Government feeds them in order to manipulate them. It is horrifying the number of people who never question or research the information the Government and other Departments feed them. Bill Gates has never vaccinated any of his own children mind you! He even come out and openly admitted that Vaccines are a part of a de population agenda (Agenda 21) and this is connected to the New World Order. The Georgian Tablets have the 10 Commandments of the New World Order written in 12 different Languages, mind you these Tablets are out in the middle of nowhere, farmland, I understand.

Chemtrails are full of poison! Aluminium, Barium, Mercury

and it would be a brilliant idea for you all to do your own research on them. The results will blow your minds severely! It is absolutely amazing the number of people who are just focused on their phones and never look up at the sky or swallow the garbage the Government spins you for why we need them. Learn to question! Stop accepting what the Government tells you as the truth, question everything, do your own research, I cannot emphasise this enough! Another reason for the Chemtrails is to block the Energy coming from the Sun which I believe, is assisting the Energies to rise here on Earth. The Illuminati don't want this happening, they want to keep us stuck in low vibrational Energy. Please do your own research!

Learn to recognise False Red Flags! There were no planes used with the Twin Towers, they were Holograms! Just think for a moment reinforced steel uprights that the "planes" were able to fly through without damaging their wings! Come on people, really! There was dynamite planted every 5 floors I understand. The steel beams were slant cut using Thermite if I remember correctly, the way they prepare buildings for demolition. One photo of Ground Zero shortly after actually showed a steel beam that had been slant cut! This was very quickly removed, both the photo and the Thermite diagonally cut steel beam.

The Twin Towers were full of Asbestos I believe, it would have cost the owners a fortune to remove it so they raised their Insurance Premiums is my understanding, shortly before the buildings were demolished! Yes people, let us call it for what really happened. Many of the Firemen reported hearing explosions but they were ignored and told to shut up! Sadly people are killed.

The Reserve Bank decide they are feeling poor so back BOTH SIDES of a War! What Countries didn't have Reserve Banks in their Countries, I believe the ones America went to war with! I understand soldiers in Afghanistan are guarding Poppy Fields, Opium people! These Countries are raped of their minerals and oil, research people!

The New World Order decided War wasn't killing off people quickly enough so Scientists manipulate the weather, it is called

HAARP! Scientists created diseases such as Aids! The only way you were going to get Ebola is if you got vaccinated I understand.

Just saw an article that suggested Cancer is a manmade disease and we have had proof that Chemotherapy is known to create Cancer! Chemotherapy was created from Agent Orange which was used in the Vietnam war.

Really makes you wonder, doesn't it? The ways the Illuminati have decided to kill off useless eaters, as they refer to us! New World Order, Agenda 21, do your own research!

There are many natural cures for Cancer, even vibration Therapy as everything vibrates at certain vibrations. This was used to cure Cancer before Big Pharma took over making Cancer Treatment creating a MULTI BILLION DOLLAR INDUSTRY!

They don't want people using natural therapies! By the way, Cancer cannot exist in an Alkaline, Oxygenated Environment. Graviola Fruit, Apricot Kernals are two things which have had excellent results in dealing with Cancer. If I was ever told I had Cancer I would use alternative therapies and stay away from Chemotherapy, Radiotherapy and Surgery if possible because it has this bad habit of spreading through your body. Personally I refuse to have Mammograms as I understand people have developed Breast Cancer from doing this.

Alkaline and oxygenate my body is what I would do

May I suggest removing as many acid forming foods from your diet as possible if you are unfortunate enough to develop Cancer. We are responsible for what we put in our mouths!

It is absolutely our choice. Are we going to eat Acidic disease creating food or Alkaline Health Promoting foods?

May I remind you of the proven Scientific fact that THOUGHTS CREATE REALITY!

If we keep telling ourselves that other members of the family have got a certain condition or sickness our sub conscious mind is extremely co – operative and will create that particular condition.

Of course some of us may choose to do the final exit home through a disease but we do choose that experience before we get here! So annoying that we don't remember making that choice. It gets very complicated when you take Past Lives and Karma into consideration. There are so many factors to take into consideration.

As a Spiritualist my understanding is that on a Soul Level, we choose to have certain experiences in this life. These experiences can be on a physical level, an emotional level, a mental level or a spiritual level. I believe that before we come here we choose how and when we are going back home and often have exit doorways we can take before the final doorway we have created. This is why people experience Near Death Experiences and their lives often change dramatically after these! Some say they have a Spiritual Awakening and become clear as to what their Life Purpose is. Many Starseeds "Wake Up" through dramatic experiences.

Others have a much slower "absorption method" such as being guided to open minded Spiritual people some of whom may practice Yoga for example.

My personal journey began in a Library, a book called The Third Eye by Tuesday Lobsang Rampa jumped out at me. Growing up a Catholic was something I had never come across beforehand but it was "calling" to me! I didn't understand how a book could call to me either but oh boy I felt like a piece of metal being drawn to a magnet! I was so hooked with curiosity! It was through reading Tuesday Lobsang Rampa's many books that I learnt about Spiritualism and there began another chapter of my life! He spoke of many fascinating natural abilities I had never heard of such as Astral Travel, Clairvoyance, Clairaudience, Clairsentience, and of course, opening your Third Eye! I felt like a camel who had been wandering the desert for decades and who had just found an Oasis at which to quench my thirst.

My journey as a Spiritualist gave me the understanding, NOTHING is ever done TO US, we create situations for our own Personal Growth! Personal Responsibility, no one to blame. The tricky part is trying to remember what the lesson was that we created the situation to learn. Something extremely challenging for us Rescuers is to ask for help. Crash and Burn assists us to do this. These lessons may be Listening, Patience, Trust, Surrender and letting go of Control. We are the only ones we have control over, our thoughts and our behaviours, never other adults or situations.

Have you ever heard of the Serenity Prayer? I found it extremely supportive, Let Go and Let God (Higher Self) or whomever you feel comfortable surrendering to for your highest guidance. As I ask, whatever is for my highest spiritual good please.

From being a catholic I took the understanding that there were Higher Beings (Angels) and that we had a Soul which survived our physical death. This took me down the pathway of well if all humans have a Soul! It doesn't matter what race, colour, religion or shoe size they have, we are ALL Children of God, because there is no way he is a human being, so as he is Spirit, we must all be Spirit as well. As the Lakota say, Mitakuye Oyasin, WE ARE ONE!

Over the years I got to meet several of my ancestors who has passed over during Evidence of Survival at Church! I am so proud of Mum, she came in 3 days after she had passed over! Her silver cord was still attached to her physical body! The first relatives to come through were my mother's Grandparents.

I had no idea who they were so the medium suggested to me that I describe them to my mother. I did and she confirmed who they were. This was a powerful moment as this was not only Evidence of Survival for me but it was Evidence of Survival for my mother as well!

In the last few days of her life I reassured her that Grandma and Grandpa would be there to meet her and they would show her how to communicate with me through Church. I was so deeply grateful to them for bringing my mother through at my original Spiritualist Church at Hughesdale. So many churches are now closing down in Tramville and my old Church was one of them. It appears that the younger members of the Congregation are unable or unwilling to carry on running the Churches.

I was very sad when Moira told me the Hughesdale Church closed down around September 2018. Tears are falling down my cheek as I write this. That Church changed my life massively for the better and began me on an amazing pathway of being of Service to Humanity through being a Psychic.

I believe it was. It was Moira and her beautiful mother Edna, who would bring me, my ten year old son and my two year old daughter to Church with them. I breast fed my daughter until she was three weeks before her third birthday. The Minister at the time, Willy, wanted me to keep her quiet so I would feed her down the back of the Church till she fell asleep. Etta Rae Smith was the founder of the Hughesdale Spiritualist Church. I was the first person to bring children into the Church. It was mainly older retired people who attended the Service.

Many years later my son married the daughter of a Spiritualist Minister who ran her own Church in Glenhuntly. I looked after her daughter through Family Day Care. Trish has medical problems so often had appointments at the Monash Medical Centre and I lived close to there. There is a fifteen year difference between Trish's mother and my son. He was only fifteen when Jennifer connected with him through a common love of Doctor Who. She was pregnant to another man who left her when she was around three months along. Anthony was the only father Daryl knew. When Daryl was seven years old they put him in a boys home according to Trish. I asked Trish what kind of father my son became, she told me he would beat up Daryl and was very hard on her as well. My understanding is that it appears he became a Narcissist just like his father. He left home at sixteen, three weeks after we had been relocated through Refuge and changed his name, and his personality also apparently. Anthony was such a beautiful psychically gifted child. He was like a big brother to the Family Day Care children I took care of. He was Clairvoyant, Clairaudient, he did automatic writing and was a Healing Channel.

Anthony's father was a Catholic as I was so both my children went to a Catholic school. Anthony went to Mazenod College. He was the smallest boy in his first year level so people got to know him real fast.

By the time he was in year ten he shut down psychically, he told me the schoolwork was too much for him. The time had come for him to begin walking down a new pathway away from his gifts, but that was a choice he had made on a Soul level before he came.

He left home three weeks after we were relocated. He enjoyed the High School he was at when we were in Refuge but apparently did not fit into the High School he attended when we were relocated.

I went to a meditation class the night he left expecting him to be home to take care of his sister. I was horrified when I got home to find that he wasn't there and she was on her own. I went to the police station to report him missing and was horrified once again when they told me they had picked him up the night before when I was at school picking his sister up. It scares me to think what he told the police to have them pick him up. Maybe he thought I was going to abuse him because his father had abused me. I grieved so deeply for my son for three years. He would ring me and hang up once I answered the phone, I just intuitively knew it was him. Several years later when I met him on the tram I asked him if indeed it had been him calling and he admitted it had. I asked him if he still connected with Peter, his brother on the other side of life and he told me he had forgotten how to do it. He used to get so cranky at me when I kept asking him what his brother was saying. Anthony would say to me, "Just open up!" I asked him how would I do that, but he couldn't tell me, so I couldn't remind him of what he used to do.

As the years rolled by and I recovered from my deep grieving at his leaving my life I was reminded of the Soul lesson I had asked him to help me to learn and that was that we do not own our children!

That was a massive lesson for me as I felt owned by my mother until the day she passed over.

It was many years before I wrapped my head around Earth being a "School of Life", where we come to learn and grow! This means of course that nothing is ever done to us! On a Soul level we create certain situations so we can learn our lessons. Sometimes these lessons are very difficult to identify so I have found that standing back from my life, like I was looking at a play, to give me a detached perspective, often helps. Of course praying / asking your Guides, angels to give you clarity is also an excellent idea!

The problem with us Rescuers is that we are major control freaks. When we wake up in the morning with an answer to a particular question that we asked the night before as we were going to sleep, and it doesn't align with what we think we want to do, then we experience massive confusion! Needing to understand confusion is created when we argue with our Guides / Angels, this goes down like a lead balloon. When we listen to our logical minds for a life choice, things always fall apart! The only thing the logical mind is good at is Maths or Science! For life's decisions our Intuition / gut feeling is what we need to listen to! Something else us Rescuers are good at doing is being stubborn, like a mule digging its hind legs into the ground figuratively speaking. Getting us to change our minds can be extremely challenging. We tend to like the status quo, change is not always something we embrace with ease. Fear of the unknown can paralyse us and often does!

The lesson of Surrender and Trust therefore is a massive one for us, it is closely linked in with not having much confidence with our own judgements. A massive lack of self-confidence due to years of being on the receiving end of emotional abuse is responsible for that!

What we need to remember is that those of us who are Psychic have had to spend nine tenths of our lives withdrawn inside ourselves because that is where it has been safe. As a consequence of this we maintain a strong connection to Spirit. Remember also, that before we reincarnate, we choose what lessons we want to learn in this life. In order for us to be "Of Service" to Humanity, we need to go through certain experiences because our clients are going through the same thing we did!

The sub conscious mind is extremely powerful people! It is a proven Scientific fact that the sub conscious fails to differentiate between Truth and a Lie and whatever you keep telling yourself is the reality you create in your life! A lot of these beliefs come from our childhoods of course from whatever our parents keep telling us which is often whatever they were told as children, it is a generational pattern such as I don't deserve, that is a very poisonous and powerful belief that a lot of us Rescuers hold onto which is behind why we run around after everyone else EXCEPT OURSELVES! The only way we become visible to ourselves is when we experience so much emotional or physical pain that we eventually ask, "What about me?" This is the breakthrough we need to begin our Emotional Healing Journey.

Whatever you keep telling yourself is what your subconscious mind creates e.g., I AM FIT AND HEALTHY! Remember we have been doing unhealthy behaviour for years as well as retaining the thought pattern that I am always sick for example, for years also, so working with the new positive thought pattern on its own is not going to work! We need to do some physical actions as well to assist creating the healthy, fit person we desire to be. Going to a gym, walking, cycling, exercising and avoiding unhealthy foods and beverages are certainly an important part in creating this new reality.

In other words, you not only have to change your "stinking thinking" but you must take physical actions towards your goal as well.

Yesterday I had the opportunity of talking to a gentleman who has had Bone Cancer for the last 4 years. He has used Vitamin B17 injections which he had to go to America to have them, and has used many other natural remedies such as Baking Soda with Maple Syrup! Cancer LOVES SUGAR so the Maple Syrup draws it in and the Baking Soda deals with the Cancer. I understand when you have Chemotherapy Treatment, they give you boiled lollies afterwards which FEEDS THE CANCER YOU ARE ATTEMPTING TO ELIMINATE!

He can only use each one for a short amount of time then needs to try something different. He has just lost his younger brother from a very aggressive blood cancer and grieving is quite a challenge for him. His brother passed over 3 weeks after he was diagnosed.

Many alternative therapy doctors have died mysteriously (I believe they have been murdered), as Cancer is a multi-billion dollar Industry and big pharma don't like their profits being taken away from them.

Louise Hay wrote a book called Know Your Body many years

ago. She attributed Thought Patterns for being responsible for many conditions. When I read it many years ago I didn't resonate with some of the thought patterns she attributed so some of the health conditions that I have. However, it may be very interesting for you to check out this book of hers, and see if you resonate with the thought patterns she attributes to your conditions.

The sub conscious mind is extremely powerful, if you think you can do something or if you cannot do something you are absolutely correct in both cases because whatever you feed the sub conscious is exactly what it creates! No, it doesn't happen instantaneously but it takes a considerable amount of time for a new thought pattern to work its way through the thick wad of old thought pattern, that you may have been holding onto for decades, before it manifests into your reality. This is a scientific fact and I have discovered this has worked in my own life! Have you heard the saying, "Patience is a virtue?", well you certainly need a ton of it to see new realities eventually manifest into your life. There is no point holding onto a new belief pattern for a weekend and then when it doesn't manifest come Monday, you think well that was a load of crock! Persistence is an integral aspect of change. It took sometimes many decades to create the reality you are experiencing so of course, it isn't going to do an 180 degree turn around in a weekend!

Not only do you have to write one page of the new reality you would like to experience every day, and I mean handwritten, not typing. Handwriting tends to connect to the subconscious best as I understand it. You also may need to change some habits. For example, if you would like an increase in financial abundance you may need to become aware of where you are spending your money and learn how to budget! Spending your money on gambling in the hope of getting rich quick rarely, if ever works to bring you the abundance you are seeking! More than often you end up losing far more money than you ever win! Chasing your losses just means you end up losing much more money! You would be much better off putting the money you put towards gambling into a separate bank account. You will be surprised how fast it grows!

You need to be practical and realistic. If you find money runs through your hands like water and you have several credit cards on the go maybe you need to pay them off and maybe even cut them up.

Be aware when you are spending and living above your means or you might find yourself with very severe financial problems. You may lose your car or worse still, your house!

The same goes for your Health. Writing one page every day, I am now fit and healthy and still overeating, drinking lots of sugary drinks and not exercising will never get you the reality you desire. Having a good look at the amount of sugar and carbohydrates you consume and the quantity of food you consume and reducing these considerably with balanced exercise you are far more likely to experience the result you wish to achieve.

Some people use food to stuff down their emotions, a better suggestion would be to get some Counselling to deal with your Inner Child work. Learn new ways to deal with generational patterns, and how to change them to have better outcomes. It is our responsibility if we do something or fail to do something, it is our own behaviour after all! We have free will. When we identify we have a weakness or need to Emotionally Heal, it is purely our responsibility as adults to seek professional help. We don't need to just rely upon ourselves if we don't have the required skills to heal.

Do some research, ask your Guides, your Higher Self, to connect you with the right people for you to support you on your Healing Journey. Us Rescuers find it very difficult to ask for help, we only know how to give! We need to become visible to ourselves and learn to receive. It is important to heal on all levels, Mental, Emotional, Physical and Spiritual.

Now many of us aren't 20 years old anymore, it took us many decades to get to a point where we are ready to heal so it isn't going to take place in a weekend, not even for the 20 year old people. Many of the patterns we carry are generational going back many generations. Society says our parents "Love us". Sadly in many cases this "love" is abuse, chaos, trauma, drama, abandonment. When we go into a relationship as adults, we are looking for tender loving care and support, but we will never find it in another until we become parents to ourselves and learn to love ourselves in this way. I am not referring to vanity rather learning to be nice to ourselves and healing negative beliefs we have picked up.

However we speak to our children becomes their inner voice which is where we got our beliefs from. We do the best we can with the understanding we grew up with. If we were perfect we wouldn't need to be here in this School of Life. We choose our parents and our children chose us! We often reincarnate in Soul Groups, playing different roles so we can learn the various lessons we have chosen. I mean, how many people do you know have learnt Patience for example? Have you? How many times have you met someone for the first time and feel like you have known them forever, even members of your own immediate family?

Whatever we are given in the first 7 years of our lives is what we tend to take on board as our "Love Equation". Sadly it is often not tender loving care and support but remember, we chose to have this experience! We don't remember karma from Past Lives, we come through the grey mists of forgetfulness.

For a reason although some of the children who have been incarnating recently seem to have been able to bring their memories with them. Mary Rodwell refers to them as the New Humans.

I have found that many of us Starseeds have come this time to tie up loose ends regarding the relationships we have had from Past Lives, tidying up any karma, so we can then connect with the people who have also been working on themselves so we can complete what we came here to do, together like a team. This has been my experience anyway. Gunter and I had a Soul Contract we needed to complete like everyone else. It is surprising how fast time has gone. This year we have been a part of each other's lives for 10 years playing various roles but mainly close friends which is a very special, powerful connection.

I can never see myself living with him full time ever again unless one of us needs to take care of the other one, to me that is different. Being able to support each other when we experience poor health is important.

Many of us Starseeds are looking for our Twin Flames, that special someone we have such a deep and powerful connection with. We don't have to live with them, we don't have to marry them. I do feel a good emotional, open communication between you is very important as mental telepathy is still not a very widely practised art as yet. Well I have recently "had my socks knocked off" hardcore! I have reconnected with my Twin Flame that I ran from for three years. He does Mental Telepathy so my mind is an open book to him! I must admit that has taken some time to get use to! I was totally shocked the other day, I heard his voice in my head! It has now happened twice to me! He suffers Industrial deafness being an Architect / builder, he also gets very distracted on his phone, so I did an experiment a couple of weeks ago. I had to leave him for a few minutes in a shopping centre, by the time I got back he was buried in his phone, big time! The thought crossed my mind to test him out to see how telepathic he was so I stood behind him and sent him the thought of "Hunny" We were both surprised, he jumped up so high with this shocked look on his face, it was priceless!

So many relationships break down because one party will assume that if the other party loves them then "they should know" what they want or why they are upset, this is a disastrous assumption.

Good communication helps us to navigate the ups and downs we experience with that special person in our lives. We will always set lessons up for ourselves for our own Personal Growth. Remember, we are all individuals and we grow Spiritually at different rates. Often we will find one partner's strengths are the other partner's weaknesses.

My Healing Journey

Over the years I have used many different Healing Modalities. Recognising we need to heal on many levels, Mental, Emotional,

Physical and Spiritual. Hate to tell you, it isn't something we can do in a weekend. I have found this Healing Journey similar to an onion in that there are many different layers we need to work through before we reach the middle of the onion, we often feel that we are repeating stuff we have already looked at but we only do a small depth every time so we don't put ourselves into overwhelm.

Doing Counselling, working on healing your Inner Child is extremely important in changing the type of people you bring into both your relationships and your friendships. Old behaviour patterns that we have held onto for decades can be extremely challenging to overcome. Fear of the unknown is a very effective emotion that stops us from moving forward into the unknown and a whole new far more self-nurturing existence. Learning to become visible to ourselves, putting up boundaries and learning a new magical word called NO is extremely challenging as is learning to receive and cutting toxic people out of our lives especially when they are family, is a massive challenge for many of us.

We often play "Blame Post" and have a massive "Guilt" button on our backs which many people in our lives are extremely good at pushing! Learning new ways of behaving is massive as we so easily slip back into old behaviour patterns without even realising it! Some of us are perfectionists and give ourselves a very hard time when we make a so called mistake. The way I understand this world as a schoolhouse for learning, means there are no such things as mistakes, only lessons we set up for ourselves to learn such as Trust (of the guidance we receive from our Higher Selves, Guides, Angels, God etc), Patience and Surrender for example. Us Rescuers who are extremely good at being invisible to ourselves have this tendency to be major Control Freaks who are very good at stress and worry over other adults behaviour or lack of it which is their responsibility NEVER OURS! We can also be very good at telling God what to do and when and of course, this NEVER works. May I suggest, every time you find yourself stressing / worrying, take a step back and ask yourself, who or what is it I am trying to control, then FORGIVE YOURSELF! Oh my goodness, I have just opened a massive can of worms here in the form of Forgiveness. Please understand when we don't forgive someone it has absolutely no effect on them but it has a massive effect on OUR HEALTH! It doesn't mean we forget what they did but in my world, NOTHING is ever done to us, we create it for our own personal growth! So bottom line, we forgive people for the sake of our own health, it has nothing to do with them!

I believe, holding onto negative emotions actually creates illness within our bodies, many books are written on this subject for example, Louise Hays, You can Heal your body. Please feel free to do your own research!

Us Rescuers need to learn, the ONLY thing we have control over is our thoughts and our behaviour! There is scientific proof that the sub conscious mind fails to differentiate between Truth and a Lie, whatever thoughts we keep feeding it is the reality the sub conscious creates! No it doesn't happen instantaneously, it can take many months as the new thought pattern needs to work its way through the thick wad of negative thoughts which you may have been holding onto since you were a child. A common belief we have carried since our childhoods is "I don't deserve", this is why we are terrible at receiving or being visible to ourselves. Sometimes we may half do things for ourselves such as buying something which is beneficial to us such as Rescue Remedy which reduces stress, but we often forget to take it. Sadly it doesn't work by osmosis.

I find having a notebook and recording every time we do "Nice" for ourselves and give ourselves a big tick, like when we were at Primary school and got a maths sum right or spelled a word correctly, how good did that tick make you feel? Be gentle with yourselves. In the first month we may only do two things for ourselves, come the end of the next month we may have added something new to the list.

Now for me, healing on a Spiritual level uses tools such as Energy Healing, Reiki, Kinesiology, Tapping. Tools which clear blockages from our Auras. Now some of these blockages, such as Abandonment, in my case (Emotional or physical unavailability or were your parents workaholics?), didn't just come from this life time but from many

Past Lives as well and I believe I have been reincarnating here for an extremely long time!

I have been extremely blessed to have connected with an extremely gifted Energy Healer for which I am deeply grateful. Now there is a bit of a twist to not only her life but to the life of a dear friend who is a powerful Healing channel herself. My Sky Family has been coming into my Healing sessions for quite a while now. Now both these ladies were quite surprised to see them come in, my Third Eye is still in the process of opening so they have described to me what my Sky Family was doing. They have even done psychic surgery on me. The Energy Healer was unable to move her hand from my knee for around 15 to 20 minutes while the surgery was taking place. Mind you I had asked then if they could do some surgery on my knee as it wanted to keep collapsing on me. I am so Blessed it hasn't done that since the surgery. As they were both witnesses to my Sky Family coming in I have asked them both to write down their experiences for me to include in this book.

I shall begin with the Energy Healer. She mentions that she had just learned how to run Barrs just before she met me so she decided to run the Barrs for me. During the Treatment she could see me change so asked me if I would like to speak. I began speaking Light Language so she had no idea what I was saying. I had connected with a Light Language Meditation Group several months beforehand, we met once a month so I had been speaking Light Language for over a year before this event. It is interesting how you are guided into these groups when the time is right. A couple of people who attended the Night Watches I attended also spoke Light Language. I remember hearing several people speak Light Language before I spoke it myself. I just had to get out of my own way and allow my Sky Family to overshadow me so I could channel them. Interesting learning curve I can tell you! As my Energy Healer couldn't understand what I was saying, she asked me to translate it into English which I did. She said my channelling was very clear and informative. She confirmed, through using her Clairvoyance, I was channelling other Beings, my Sky Family. During the Treatments, most of the Healing was channelled through her from my Sky Family. She could see lots of information being downloaded into me. Lots of Energy gridding going on through my body which she found very exciting to watch. Most of the sessions she could have sat in the corner and watched as they were doing all the work. She feels very privileged to have my Sky Family come into the Healing Sessions I was having there. Her vibrations were obviously high enough for her to be a conduit also and for them to be able to come into this very heavy and low density for them. She observed me grow more comfortable and confident within myself.

My girlfriend had a very interesting experience with me on the way home one day. I experienced "Missing Time" whilst driving the car! I trust my Sky Family totally, they always look after me when I am driving. Anyway, they decided they hadn't finished working on me before I left so decided to yank me and bring in a replacement to drive the car. My poor girlfriend turned around to speak to me and as she is Clairvoyant, she could see my soul wasn't in my body but someone else was there. She hadn't experienced anything like that before so she was a bit surprised when it happened, it was quite an experience for her but she knew we were in safe hands. We were not the only ones in my car that day either! When I came back it was like, how did I get here?

Actually it was in Couldville doing a mini "Vision Quest", hiking up to the Birthing Cave, where I had my first experience of Missing Time. I had been given a walking stick to use. I arrived at the Medicine Wheel at the base of the cave and suddenly I realised I didn't have my stick. I was really confused as to where it was! It was not until I was walking back to Jim's car with the guidance of Mr O'Mara, that I realised there were huge areas I had no memory of walking through. It really spun me out and I was so grateful Bill had agreed to stay with me or I would have been severely lost!

I had experienced missing time before one day when my daughter was driving me home with my eldest grandson. There was a little mini made up as a panel van right in front of us with a wee ladder on the roof and we were having a deep discussion on how on earth could a toolbox fit in the back. I might add, before we left her place we were discussing UFO's.

She was very skeptical about them. My theory is my Sky Family decided to step in and show her that unexplained occurrences do happen, We were about to turn right onto a busy street. Next thing we knew we were a good 25 minutes down the road in heavy traffic. My grandson spoke asking how did the little mini get to be 10 cars in front of us. I realised we had experienced missing time, it blew my daughter's mind so severely she buried that event so deeply into her mind, she couldn't explain it, plus, she was driving and it freaked her out so badly!

It was mind blowing enough to experience "Missing Time" when someone else was driving the car but it is a whole different situation when you are driving the car and having the experience.

Now I know how my daughter felt that day. She has no concept of Sky Family. It wasn't as "freaky" for me as I am very aware of my Sky Family keeping me safe on the roads.

Missing Time can be experienced in many other scenarios as well for example when you are reading a book and you realise several hours have gone by and you thought you had been reading for an hour. When you are really enjoying yourself, I find time seems to pass extremely quickly but of course when you are waiting for something exciting to happen, oh boy! It seems to drag really severely!

I have an understanding that there is no such thing as time, that it is purely a manmade concept. Apparently, according to Quantum Physics, we actually live in the Eternal NOW! That took quite a while for me to get my head around, never mind the multi-dimensional Time Lines that we are existing in all at the same time. !

Personally that is a massive concept for me but there are some people who remember so called Past Lives, who seem to have the ability to jump Time Lines. Now I know that for many of you this may sound more Science Fiction than fact and I totally understand why you would feel that way as it is such a mind blowing concept! I suppose it made it easier to understand once I had experienced my own "Missing Time". Does this make any sense to those of you who have had it also?

It is my understanding that when I am asleep I spend time up on my Ship, the Neptune, which I have been told I am a Lieutenant Commander. The Neptune is the Pleiadian Flag Ship! She is three miles high, three miles wide and thirty miles long! When my girlfriend Tina, asked me what the name of my Ship was my logical mind went, "What the?" I was still trying to wrap my head around being told I was a Lieutenant Commander! My mind went blank for what seemed like ages then out to my right, like someone was standing next to me speaking, because the voice I heard was outside my head. Oh boy, that was a first! I had never experienced Clairaudience before! Once I told Tina the name, she quickly Googled it and discovered five channellings of it! That really surprised me massively! I think I was more shocked by the fact she had confirmed that there was indeed a Ship / UFO, by that name!

Personally I have no memory of being there just a "knowing" if that makes sense to any of you. I also believe I spend time with my Hybrid Children while I am there. I have a friend on FB, Leah, who is aware of her Hybrid kids, she is Clairvoyant! They are more ET than human so they cannot exist down here, although I do understand there are some that are more human that do exist down here. I have an understanding that perhaps they do not survive for long.

I do believe however there are many ET's walking around on Earth, blending in like chameleons!

I have been told my memory of being on the Ship is left on the Ship so I cannot get hijacked for them.

I understand many people have memories, or screen memories given to them of their time on board the Ships. Some are shown a timeline where the Earth is being destroyed for example and are being told that is what will happen if we continue with certain behaviours here.

In my understanding us Starseeds have been chosen to assist Mother Earth and the humans to Ascend into the 5th Dimension like we have assisted many other planets to do! Mother Earth is the last piece of the puzzle to go in so the whole sector can Ascend. This is my understanding. I do believe there will be two Earths eventually, a 3D Earth like we have now where all the lower vibrational energies will be confined to and a 5D Earth where Love, Peace and Harmony will reign. I am so looking forward to being in 5D where thoughts are instantaneously transformed into reality which is why no lower vibrational energies can exist there! I have come to the understanding that both the 3D and 5D Earths will co-exist in the same space, just inhabiting the different vibrations so 3D people will be unaware of the 5D Earth. My understanding is that all instantaneous wars, hate, violence, judgement, prejudice etc, that will remain in the 3D world.

Personally I am really looking forward to a world of Peace, Harmony and Unconditional Love. I am more than ready to release this world of Duality. Yes we created it to learn lessons, that is my understanding.

Speaking of Peace and Harmony I would like to do a little deviation as today is Anzac Day

War, a New World Order Agenda

Remember, this is my personal belief, I mean no disrespect to all those innocent souls who have lost their lives in war and to all those who were injured, physically and mentally, or to the families who lost members due to wars. In my opinion wars are EVIL! They are a part of the New World Order de population Agenda 21.

Are you aware that the Federal Reserve backs BOTH SIDES of EVERY WAR? They make money through war! Are you as shocked as I was when I first learned about this? I found it extremely challenging for me to believe this until, through David Icke's videos, he explained what is really happening through interviewing high level whistle blowers!

Recently David was refused entry into Australia! He has been here many times before, those in power must be getting very concerned because people are waking up and realising that David has been telling us the TRUTH over the last 25 years or so. Those in power did not expect David to have so many followers. As long as people thought he was crazy the people in power were not concerned!

So much for freedom of speech in Australia, that seems to be severely restricted now!

I have noticed on FB, several posts are now being removed and even on YouTube, there are certain videos which we can no longer watch! There is a lot of censorship happening!

Many posts are now beginning to come up on FB of people waking up to the lies behind the creation of wars. They are noticing that one main country has begun many of the wars in the preceding decades over false claims.

It is now surfacing the true reasons they have gone to war was related to these countries not having a Federal Reserve Bank, they had oil, minerals etc that this particular country decided they wanted for themselves!

We need to understand the Illuminati / Cabal are some of the richest families in the world who select who the people in power are going to be! Presidents are selected by these people, not elected by the people!

The two political parties are nothing more than the two wings of the same bird! This is of course, the New World Order! The people behind this I believe are a bunch of Sociopaths, Psychopaths and Narcissists who have absolutely no Empathy whatsoever! The first goal of the New World Order is to kill off many people and enslave the rest. They even erected stone tablets in the middle of a field, Georgian Tablets I believe they were referred to. The 10 Commandments of the New World Order were written in 12 different languages on this stone tablet. There were photos of it on FB, there is still information about them on Google and You Tube so please feel free to research this yourselves.

War wasn't killing off people as fast as they would like. There was a post on FB where Bill Gates has admitted his vaccines were created with depopulation as the purpose. I am led to understand Bill Gates refuses to vaccinate his own children! Anybody else finding this a bit suspicious?

Chemtrails, spraying us with nasty substances are being very effective in making people sick and killing many. Chemotherapy and Big Pharma medications kill many people as well. Medications with their secondary effects, then doctors give them medication for those effects and so the ripple grows.

I believe that Scientists have created diseases and I believe Cancer is one of them. Aids and Ebola I believe have also been deliberately created by scientists. Strange, nobody is speaking about Ebola anymore, that disappeared very quickly. My understanding was, the only way you were going to get Ebola was being vaccinated. You just have to look at the ingredients in vaccines. Apparently the insert list is very big! Now where else are these being used? Barium and Aluminium are being used in Chemtrails, how interesting.

David Icke speaks of non-physical beings called Archons. He has done many years research regarding them and found references to them in a variety of places and by various different names. He refers to the way these beings manipulate certain low vibrational humans is like the way scientists will have a dangerous substance in a container, and they will stand on the outside of the container, and place their hands into gloves which go within the container, and then manipulate whatever they are doing with the use of these gloves. The Archons can only manipulate humans with a level of Reptilian DNA of 50% or greater which is why these humans intermarry within their own group to keep the DNA undiluted otherwise the Archons are unable to manipulate them. These people need to have no Empathy which Narcissists, Sociopaths and Psychopaths have in common.

Untruthfulness, insincerity, lack of remorse and shame (Politicians and Lawyers) immediately come to mind when you mention untruthfulness to me connecting to people with powerful positions, how about you? Do you relate to this as well? David mentions these Archons feed of FEAR so they are continually manipulating situations to create as much of it as they can. During war they have a full on banquet!

I don't know about you but my personal mission is to "Starve" these entities by living my life in Peace and Harmony and sending them LOVE which is like poison to them! They rely on humanity staying in low vibrations of fear, hate, anger, judgement, prejudice etc. so they have an ample supply of negative emotions to feed off. Let us all work on ourselves and monitor the energy we are sending to them! Raise your vibrations to Love, Peace, Harmony, Joy and Happiness and starve these Archons! In my understanding, we are ALL children of God, no matter what label we give to him, it is irrelevant.

Even science is now discovering we are not just flesh and blood but Spirit and in my terminology, we are Spirit having a human experience. We come to learn lessons of Surrender, Trust (especially of our own intuition), Patience, Forgiveness (understand when we don't forgive someone it isn't affecting them in the least but oh boy, it is destroying our mental and emotional health).

Surrendering to whomever we acknowledge as the Highest Spiritual power in our lives, remembering to ask for help and guidance when we need it. Patience, oh boy, that is another huge lesson especially for control freaks. When you find yourself getting stressed or worried, believe me, you are either trying to control another adults behaviour or a situation, neither of which are ours to control!

With Trust, being able to trust ourselves, listening to our own intuition and stop second guessing ourselves. When we go by what we analyse, everything always falls apart on us and we are sitting there scratching our heads wondering why it didn't work out. Sometimes we get an answer to do something else than what we thought we wanted to do and it is a real challenge to let go of what we thought we needed to do and go with the guidance we have received. Everything always works out what is meant to be when we listen and act on our guidance.

You see, in my world, as a Spiritualist, I believe we choose what lessons we want to learn before we get here but that memory is wiped from our minds when we come through the grey mists of forgetfulness. As far as I understand, thought creates reality is a proven scientific fact. For example the thought," I don't deserve, nothing ever works out for me" creates some very challenging situations. The thought," I cannot trust" finds us surrounded by untrustworthy people. The upside of this is WE are the ones in charge of our thought patterns so we can change them and create a whole new reality! Often we have been holding onto negative thought patterns since childhood. One way of identifying what thought patterns we are creating is to grab a pen and paper and sit back and just observe your thought patterns and write down the negative ones. Then we turn them around to positive thoughts in the present tense, such as "I now have Peace and Harmony within me and around me".

I ignore the logical mind going," well that is a big fat lie", when we are dealing with life decisions. When we are working with the sub conscious mind that doesn't know the difference between the truth and a lie, we need to remember it creates a new reality over several months. Remember, we have been holding onto the negative thought for decades sometimes. A new positive reality needs time to work its way through that thick wad of negative thought patterns, before it can manifest into this reality! Personally I have found using Rescue Remedy drops, creams, sprays or lozenges very useful for dissolving stress from my aura and bringing me back into calmness. May crystals, essential oils and incenses also help bring back calmness. I just love using white sage, burning it in a Paua shell, and focusing on the corners in my home. Negative energies / entities love to hide in corners!

I advise clients to write one page every day of what the new reality is they wish to experience, such as I now have peace and harmony within me and around me thank you. The reason we hand write this is that is how we connect to our sub conscious mind to create the new reality we desire. Using Gratitude is a very powerful too! Practice identifying three things you are Grateful for every day, especially if your energy is flat and you are feeling depressed, angry, frustrated, resentful etc.

Living in an attitude of Gratitude really expands positive energy.

Patience plays a major role in manifesting, there is no point in writing the new reality you want for a week then going, this is a load of rubbish, it didn't work! You need to remember how long you have been holding onto the old thought patterns and allow the new thought pattern to work its way through the thick wad of old thought pattern to manifest into the present time for you.

Many of us are carrying Poverty Consciousness and Abandonment issues, these will take many years to heal as we have often experienced these situations in Past Lives as well.

Regarding our poverty consciousness and our abandonment issues is a powerful belief system which states, "I don't deserve". See how something simple can have massive effects on many levels in our lives.

As these issues are so massive we need to accept professional assistance to deal with them, unfortunately many of us have massive issues with receiving so asking for help is a massive issue for us. The kookaburras are laughing at me because they know it has been a massive issue of mine as well, how timely for them to do that.

Many of us are perfectionists and tend to give ourselves a hard time whenever we make a mistake; (refresher course here, there is no such thing as a mistake, purely a lesson, that we ourselves, on a soul level, created so we could learn and grow). Be gentle with yourselves, put that energetic club down and stop hitting yourself over the head with it!

If we were perfect, we wouldn't need to be here. When you were a child, who said to you," Not good enough, do it again?" Where they stopped, we took over. Then we have the other extreme, the "Blamers" who never take responsibility for anything they did or failed to do. One thing we need to keep in mind is that the only adults behaviour we are responsible for is OUR OWN! Some of us run around like headless chickens after other people so we don't have to look at our own hurt and pain.

Now coming back to War, who is it that sends all these Patriotic young men and women off to war using false claims? They don't care about these beautiful people being killed or more recently innocent women and children. They are all seen as casualties of war now aren't they! How cold hearted, greedy and manipulative these people are in my eyes. Have you noticed it seems to be all the poor people who get to do the dirty work of fighting and getting killed! Never the rich Illuminati kids. They would be the ones in charge, probably not on the front lines so much. Forgive me, I know nothing about war, it makes me sick just thinking about it!

They used Conscription for Vietnam and objectors were imprisoned or classed as mentally ill. They didn't care about the broken families, although in setting up Leagues Clubs they pretended to care but look at all the war veterans living on the streets in America without a home. All the empty houses in America due to Bank foreclosures I understand getting run down because nobody is living there and taking care of them. In my view there is something terribly wrong with this situation.

Another horrendous situation is the CEO of Nestle saying Humans do not deserve free water. Does anyone else find this statement unusual? Maybe he is artificial intelligence part robot / machine and part human, maybe that would explain his attitude. Personally I will be boycotting Nestle products due to this, anyone else with me?

Sociopaths and Psychopaths are two other very dangerous groups of people! Beware, some of these people hold very high positions of office! They are all about Service to self, greed and they don't care about anybody else. Oh they are very good at pretending they may care but please take notice, actions speak louder than words! Often they say one thing then do the complete opposite but sadly Fluoride Sulphate has dumbed down so many people that those in high positions simply are not questioned with the garbage that comes out their mouths!

How many of you are aware that the Reserve bank finances BOTH sides of every war! Shocked are you? Please feel free to do your own research! David Icke is a brilliant source of unspoken Truth of what goes on behind the scenes. He takes you way, way down the rabbit hole so hold onto your hats folks and be prepared to open your mind, it is like a parachute, it works best when it is open.

He has heaps of videos on You Tube and he has released several books as well. We are never too old to learn the Truth of what is going on behind the scenes! It will so severely blow your mind, so be prepared. Allow your mind to be a sponge, accept what resonates with you and discard the rest. If you come back to it a year later you may be ready to learn some more that you were not comfortable in wrapping your head around.

David has done a couple of wonderful videos talking about the Archons. He has researched this subject in depth and speaks of the Religions, Secret Societies, Satanism and the Archon's need for Ritual. They have absolutely no empathy so can carry out horrendous acts, such as Pedophelia, murder and carry out ritualistic Human sacrifices without a care in the world. He alerts us to the fact these beings use our energy as food, not any energy however. The main energies they delight in are Fear, Anger, Hate, Judgement, Resentment, Racial Prejudice, Rage, Bullying. Anything that creates separation, the more negative, the greater their feast! They totally thrive on these negative energies! Now, how would you make sure you had a continual food supply? Hey horror / murder movies, that sounds like a good source, how about wars, now a lot of people are affected by them! so these Archons have an absolute feast during times of war! They don't want us to live in Peace and Love, they would starve! I say, let us starve these Archons by expanding our Love vibrations for everyone on Mother Earth!

The Arcons rely on us remaining divided, judging, hating each other. The Lakota have a beautiful saying, Mitakuye Oyasin, loosely translated means," We are one!"

The Arcons certainly do not want us waking up to the fact we are all Spirit having a human journey.

How would it feel to you if we treated each other how we would like to be treated? I have a suggestion, how about we focus on joy, laughter, happiness and Love as these energies raise the vibrations on Mother Earth. Learn to Nurture Ourselves, us Rescuers are so good at being invisible to ourselves. It is so beautiful how our fur babies, our cats and dogs, give us unconditional love when we are kind to them. What an amazing world we would live in if we all treated each other with this same kindness. Remember, we are not responsible for other adults' behaviour, only our own!

Sadly Narcissists, Psychopaths and Sociopaths are wired very differently to us normal people.

They seem to thrive on hurting or harming other people or animals. What we need to understand is that these people will never change! We can never fix them and they will never fix themselves!

Every night I do a practice of sending Healing Energy for Mother Earth and for everyone in need of Healing. I even include pets when I am doing this. What an amazing world it would be if all the beautiful caring people on Earth all joined in with this using Prayer / Meditation, Visualisations, whatever way that resonates with them with the intent to bring Peace, Harmony and Healing to Mother Earth and all upon her. Maybe we could all use our imaginations and visualise a blanket of Love surrounding Mother Earth and all who live upon her.

MITAKUYE OYASIN – WE ARE ONE!

ACKNOWLEDGEMENTS

Firstly, I want to thank the loved one that gave the Medium the message that I was required to write this book about my life. I also want to thank the Medium responsible for bringing the message through, I did not understand why people would be interested in hearing about the journey my life had been, there had been so much pain involved.

I began writing this after I was relocated from Refuge, my daughter turned 8 years old in Refuge and my son had left home at 16 years old, three weeks after we had been relocated. Third time successful after two false starts, it is finally completed! My daughter is now 33.

I was in massive pain! Let us not forget that his father had threatened to kill me and burn my home to the ground.

I want to thank Tuesday Lobsang Rampa for introducing me to the Spiritualist Church through his books.

Hughesdale is my home Church and I am deeply grateful to Moira and Edna for bringing me and my two children to Church.

Next I want to thank my Sky Family and my loved ones on the other side of life for all the help and support they have given me on this very long journey.

I want to thank all the people in my life for playing the roles I asked them to, on a Soul level, so I could learn the lessons I have chosen to learn. My deepest thanks to Michael for playing such a challenging role for me so I could have the experience I needed to do the work I have chosen to do. I could not possibly be a Lighthouse for others coming up behind me if it had not been for the experiences I had in that relationship.

Gunter, I deeply appreciate the journey we have had together. We had a Soul Contract to complete. We have experienced many Past Lives together and you will always have a place in my heart. Thank you for the lessons you have taught me over the past 11 years.

Tina, my most Precious SiStar, I am so blessed and deeply grateful our Sky Family connected us in Couldville in 2012. Our Soul connection is extremely deep, we have known each other for many Past Lives. I am thankful for the support we have given each other over the past 7 years. We will be there for each other for Eternity! Your unconditional love and support has been appreciated so very much.

Dinny Hopa, my beautiful Maori girlfriend, you introduced me to the UFO's and our Sky Family. You will always be in my heart, you taught me much, thank you. I hear your voice in my head every time I read the word, "realm". I love you and miss you greatly, I know you are just a thought away however.

Theo Raaymaakers, thank you for reconnecting me to the Good Red Road and my Native American Past Lives. I connect very powerfully to the Native American way of life, their traditions and ceremonies. I feel deeply connected to the Hunkpapa Lakota Sioux. Shakina Blue Star, a Lakota Medicine Woman, channelled my Grandfather from Past Life in the old language. Tatanka Iotanka (Sitting Bull). She did a Psychic drawing of him and gave me my Hunkpapa name of Little Feather, I am a member of the Eagle Clan.

Brita Hollows, you introduced me to En-jah, my Mantid Surgeon who did my Spinal surgery energetically, then guided the surgeon's hands. He also assisted with my knee replacement surgery. I am deeply grateful to him.

Russ, thank you for all the assistance you gave me with transferring files for my book and for taking care of me with Mobility equipment. His business is, MOBILITY AND YOU, located at;

3/675 Deception Bay Road
Deception Bay, Qld, 4508
1300 366 096
www.mobilityandyou.com.au

ABOUT THE AUTHOR

She grew up a Catholic in a State School during the thirty year war in Ireland between the Catholics and the Protestants. This made her wonder what the common denominator between all Christians was as they all seemed to interpret the bible differently. Later on she searched to find the common denominator underneath all religions. She came to the conclusion that we were all Spirit having a human experience in this School of Life. It was irrelevant what Nationality, skin color, Race or Religion we were, were were not our physical body, that was just an overcoat we wear while here on Earth. She concluded, like the Lakota Sioux say, Mitakuye Oyasin; all our relations. We are One in her view, just having different lessons to learn while we are here. She believes everything happens for a reason, she refers to these as life lessons which we create for our own personal growth. Another favorite say of hers is, "Nothing happens until the time is right", not in our time as we would prefer. Patience is a very challenging lesson indeed, one she has struggled with on many occasions. As Rescuers, we tend to be "control freaks", wanting things to happen now, or yesterday even! How many of you can relate to that?

Printed in the United States
By Bookmasters